"十二五"江苏省高等学校重点教材（教材编号2015-2-069）

畅游江苏

WALKING AROUND JIANGSU

主编 黄华 马嵘

编委 陈菲 徐华 蒋芸 谢颖

南京大学出版社

图书在版编目(CIP)数据

畅游江苏 = Walking Around Jiangsu / 黄华,马嵘

主编. — 南京 :南京大学出版社,2016.6

ISBN 978-7-305-17240-3

Ⅰ.①畅… Ⅱ.①黄… ②马… Ⅲ.①旅游指南-江

苏省 Ⅳ.①K928.953

中国版本图书馆 CIP 数据核字(2016)第 146657 号

出版发行 南京大学出版社

社　　址 南京市汉口路 22 号　　　　　邮　编 210093

出 版 人 金鑫荣

书　　名 畅游江苏(WALKING AROUND JIANGSU)

主　　编 黄 华 马 嵘

责任编辑 刁晓静　　　　　　　编辑热线 025-83592123

照　　排 南京南琳图文制作有限公司

印　　刷 南京鸿图印务有限公司

开　　本 787×1092 1/16 印张 13 字数 427 千

版　　次 2016 年 6 月第 1 版 2016 年 6 月第 1 次印刷

ISBN 978-7-305-17240-3

定　　价 66.00 元

网址:http://www.njupco.com

官方微博:http://weibo.com/njupco

微信服务号:njuyuexue

销售咨询热线:(025)83594756

前　言

　　与经济全球化相伴相生的教育国际化,不仅使地球成为一个村落,也让各种文明有更多的机会在同一时空交相辉映。今天的中国,因为悠久的历史文化、安定的社会环境、蓬勃的经济发展、广阔的市场前景和友好的百姓民众,正在吸引越来越多的外国留学生、国际交流人士和外国旅游者。

　　江苏地处中国东部,历史悠久,风光秀丽,民风淳朴,经济繁荣,教育发达。江苏的发展从一个侧面反映了中国的发展,江苏的文化从一个角度体现了中国文化的博大精深。

　　本教材力图通过简洁易懂、图文并茂、英汉对照的方式呈现江苏的历史、地理、文化、经济、旅游、城市特色以及民俗特点。教材以江苏文化为切入点,力求以景寓文,生动有趣,通过精选的城市、景点及传统文化载体突出对江苏文化资源的解读,同时适当拓展至更丰富的中国文化,增强学习者对中国文化尤其是江苏文化的理解力。教材统分结合,各单元既有联系又具有一定的独立性,章节内容可以根据需要进行二次组合。教材既有利于引导留学生及来苏国际交流人士了解江苏、认同江苏、喜爱江苏,也适合旅游类专业涉外人员宣传江苏、推广江苏,让更多的人成为江苏文化的目击者、体验者与传播者。

　　本教材由在国际合作与交流领域、跨文化应用与传播方面有丰富经验的专业人员,旅游专业一线教师,以及旅游行业尤其是在国际旅游业资深的专业人士跨界联合编写而成。扬州工业职业技术学院黄华负责教材框架和章节的设计;南京科技职业学院马嵘负责教材内容和课件范式的设计。本教材共设三篇。第一篇由扬州工业职业技术学院黄华编写;第二篇第一章由南京科技职业学院马嵘编写;第二篇第二章和第三篇第四章由扬州工业职业技术学院陈菲编写;第二篇第三章和第三篇第二章由扬州工业职业技术学院谢颖编写;第二篇第四章第一节和第三篇第三章由扬州工业职业技术学院徐华编写;第二篇第四章第二节和第三篇第一章由南京科技职业学院蒋芸编写。南京国际翻译导游公司王飞华总经理对教材中旅游资源的选择给予了具体指导。本教材受到"江苏省高校青蓝工程"资助。

　　国外高校对留学生的文化类课程教育早已开设。相比之下,国内的此类课程才刚刚起步。再加上编者水平有限,难免有不少错谬之处,恳请大家批评指正。

编　者

2016 年 4 月

Preface

With the globalization of the world's economy, education becomes increasingly international. Our modern world is a global village, which offers more opportunities for all cultures to exchange and shine at the same time. Thanks to a long history and rich culture, nowadays China is in an increasingly stable social environment and experiencing rapid economic development. Vast market prospects and friendly people are attracting more and more foreign students to study here. These days, China has become the destination for international exchange and new experience.

The Province of Jiangsu is located in Eastern China. It boasts a long history, beautiful scenery, quaint local customs, economic prosperity and advanced education. To some extent, the development of Jiangsu reflects the development of China, and Jiangsu culture reflects the extensive and profound Chinese culture.

This book employs both English and Chinese to display Jiangsu's history, geography, culture, economy, tourism, cities and folk customs, to make it more interesting. Taking Jiangsu's culture as an example, the book strives to make an interpretation of cultural resources in Jiangsu. We will introduce scenic spots, cities, attractions, and traditional culture. Meanwhile, the abundance of Chinese culture is covered to improve learners' understanding of China's culture, especially Jiangsu's culture. The book is a combination of general and specific information, and each unit is connected as well as independent from each other. The contents could be reorganized and combined when necessary. The book is not only suitable to help international exchange students understand and identify with Jiangsu but also appropriate for tourism personnel involved with foreign affairs to promote Jiangsu.

The book is jointly compiled by experienced international personnel, professors of cross-cultural communication, first-line teachers in Tourism, and professionals in the international tourism industry. Huang Hua, the chief editor from Yangzhou Polytechnic Institute, is responsible for the design of the framework and chapters. Ma Rong, from Nanjing Polytechnic Institute, is responsible for the structure of the content and the design of the multimedia course-ware. The book consists of three parts. Part One is written by Huang Hua. The first chapter of Part Two is written by Ma Rong. The second chapter of Part Two and the forth chapter of Part Three are

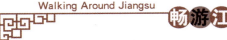

written by Chen Fei from Yangzhou Polytechnic Institute. The third chapter of Part Two and second chapter of Part Three are written by Xie Ying from Yangzhou Polytechnic Institute. The first unit of Chapter Four of Part Two and the third Chapter of Part Three are written by Xu Hua from Yangzhou Polytechnic Institute. The second unit of Chapter Four of Part Two and the first chapter of Part Three are written by Jiang Yun from Nanjing Polytechnic Institute. Wang Feihua，the General Manager of Nanjing International Translation Company，is responsible for the guidance and selection of tourism resources. The book is sponsored by Jiangsu Qinglan Project.

Cultural courses have long been offered in foreign universities for international students. However，such courses in our country are just starting from scratch. We are proud to be a pioneer in this field and would also greatly appreciate your advice and suggestions. Thank you!

Editors
April 2016

目　录

第三篇　传统文化

Contents

Part Three   Traditional Culture

第一篇　江苏概览
Part One　Jiangsu Profile

中华人民共和国,简称中国,位于亚洲东部,太平洋西岸。陆地面积约960万平方公里,是世界国土面积第三大的国家。人口数量13.6782亿(2014年),是世界上人口最多的国家。首都为北京,省级行政区划为23个省、5个自治区、4个直辖市、2个特别行政区,是一个以汉族为主体民族,由56个民族构成的统一多民族国家。中国是四大文明古国之一,有着5000年悠久的历史,创造了对世界具有很大影响的四大发明:造纸术、指南针、火药及印刷术。中国是世界第二大经济体,与英、法、美、俄并列为联合国安理会五大常任理事国。

江苏,简称"苏",省会南京。公元1667年因江南省东西分置而建省,得名于"江宁府"与"苏州府"之首字。位于中国大陆东部沿海中心,地处富饶美丽的长江三角洲。

江苏省的简称"苏"的繁体字"蘇"由草、水、鱼、禾四个汉字组成,象征着江苏自古就是鱼米之乡。江苏省经济繁荣、教育发达、文化昌盛。江苏是中国古代文明的发祥地之一,拥有吴、金陵、淮扬、中原四大多元文化。江苏地跨长江、淮河南北,京杭大运河从中穿过。江苏的城市大多依水而建,因水而繁荣。江苏的水造就了7座中国历史文化名城:南京、苏州、常熟、扬州、镇江、淮安和徐州。江苏综合经济实力在中国一直处于前列,以外向型经济为主。在2015年中国城市GDP排行榜中,江苏是唯一所有省辖市都跻身全国百强的省份。

China, the People's Republic of China, is located in eastern Asia, on the west coast of the Pacific Ocean. China is about 9.6 million square kilometers in size, the world's third largest country. China is the world's most populous country, with about 1,367,820,000 people (2014). Beijing is the capital of the country. There are 23 provinces, 5 autonomous regions, 4 municipalities directly under the central government, and 2 Special Administrative Regions. China is a unified multiethnic country, which is composed of 56 ethnic groups with the majority being the Han people. China is one of the world's most ancient civilizations, with over 5,000 years of history. Four great and worldly influential inventions were first created by Chinese ancient people including paper-making, compass, gunpowder and printing. China is the world's second largest economy, and one of the five permanent members of the UN Security Council with Britain, France, the United States and Russia.

Su is short for Jiangsu. Nanjing is the capital city of Jiangsu Province. Jiangsu gets

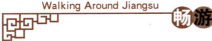

his name from the first Chinese characters of Jiangning Government Office and the Suzhou Government Office respectively，due to the establishment division of the province in 1667. Jiangsu Province is located in the center of China's eastern coast on the abundant and beautiful Yangtze River Delta.

The Chinese character "蘇（Su）" in Jiangsu is composed of grass，water，fish and crop，which best displays the image of Jiangsu, the ancient "land of plenty." Jiangsu Province has reached great achievements in economy，education and culture. As one of the birthplaces of China's ancient civilizations, Jiangsu has four great cultures, namely Wu, Jinling, Huaiyang and Zhongyuan. Jiangsu extends across the Yangtze River, North and South of Huaihe River，with the Grand Canal passing through. Most cities are built beside waters, and prosper because of water. Thus, seven historical cultural cities were developed, including Nanjing, Suzhou, Changshu, Yangzhou, Zhenjiang, Huai'an and Xuzhou. Jiangsu ranks high in the comprehensive economic power in China，based on an export-oriented economy. In the 2015 Report of China's City GDP Rankings，Jiangsu was the only province with all provincial-level cities listed into the Top 100.

第一章　地理特征
Chapter One　Geographical Features

文化贴士1

　　江苏辖江临海，平原辽阔，湖泊众多。江苏是著名的"水乡"，省内河川交错，水网密布，海岸线长 954 公里，长江横穿东西 425 公里，京杭大运河纵贯南北 718 公里，有大小湖泊 290 多个，湖泊面积达 6 260 平方公里，水域面积占 16.9%，水域比例全国最大，是全国唯一一个**江海河湖**①俱全的省份。江苏地形以平原为主，平原面积达 7 万多平方公里，占全省总面积 69%，居中国各省首位。

　　江苏地理上跨越南北，属于温带向亚热带的过渡性气候，气候温和，雨量适中，四季气候分明。

　　Jiangsu's geography is mainly plains, rivers and lakes. Jiangsu is famous as a land of rivers and lakes. There are 954 kilometers of coastline. The Yangtze River crosses 425 kilometers from West to East，and the Beijing-Hangzhou Grand Canal runs through 718 kilometers. There are over 290 lakes with 6,260 square kilometers of lake area, which accounts for 16.9% and ranks first across China. Jiangsu is the only province with river, stream, sea and lake in China. Jiangsu is mainly consisted of plains, with over 70,000 square kilometers of plain area, covering 69% of its vital area and ranks first among China's provinces.

　　Jiangsu geographically extends across northern and southern China，belonging to the subtropical transitional climate. It has a mild climate，with moderate rainfall and four distinctive seasons.

① 江是长江，世界第三大河；海是黄海；河是古运河；湖是太湖、洪泽湖。

It refers to the Yangtze River, the third longest in the world; the Yellow Sea; the Ancient Grand Canal; Taihu Lake, Hongze Lake.

 　地理位置 Location

　　江苏位于中国大陆东部沿海，介于东经 116°18′～121°57′，北纬 30°45′～35°20′之间。江苏东临黄海与太平洋，与上海市、浙江省、安徽省、山东省接壤，江苏与上海、浙江、安徽共同构成的长江三角洲城

思考 Question

找找位于同一纬度的国家和地区。

Please find other countries and areas located at the same latitude as Jiangsu.

市群已成为国际 6 大世界级城市群之一。

Jiangsu is located along the eastern coast of China between east longitude 116°18′ and 121°57′, north latitude 30°45′ and 35°20′. With the Yellow Sea and the Pacific Ocean to its east, Jiangsu adjoins Anhui and Shandong Provinces in the west and north respectively, with Zhejiang Province and the city of Shanghai as its neighbors in the southeast, which form the urban agglomeration on the Yangtze River Delta as one of the six largest metropolises in the world.

二 面积 Area

江苏省地处富饶的长江三角洲。面积 10.26 万平方公里,占中国国土面积的 1.06%。

Located in the beautiful and prosperous Yangtze River Delta, Jiangsu Province covers an area of 102,600 square kilometers, about 1.06% of the total area of the country.

三 气候 Climate

思考 Question

说说你所在国家或者城市的气候如何?

What is the climate in your home country or city like?

江苏位于中国东部,地理上跨越南北,气候、植被也同样具有南方和北方的特征,四季分明,冬冷夏热,春温多变,秋高气爽。

Jiangsu is located in eastern China, geographically crossing the north and south, as well as having the climate and vegetation from both regions. It maintains four distinct seasons, with hot summers and cold winters.

梅雨:初夏江淮流域一带经常出现一段持续较长的阴沉多雨天气。此时,器物易霉,故亦称"霉雨",简称"霉";又值江南梅子黄熟之时,故亦称"梅雨"或"黄梅雨"。

Plum Rain appears in the Yangtze River and Huaihe River in summer, for a longer period of cloudy and rainy weather. At this time, artifacts are easy to be mildewed, so it also gets known as "tsuyu," referred to as "bad"; Meanwhile, it is at the time of plums getting ripen, so it also known as "Meiyu" or "Huangmei Yu."

地形 Topography

江苏地形以平原为主,主要有淮北、淮南和江南三大平原。

The geography of Jiangsu is largely plains, consisting of the Huaibei Plain, the Huainan (South Jiangsu) Plain, and the Eastern Seashore Plain.

江苏是中国地势最低的一个省分,绝大部分地区在海拔 50 米以下。连云港云台山玉女峰为江苏最高峰,海拔624.4 米。

Jiangsu is the lowest lying area in China, and most areas are less than 50 meters above sea level. While Yunv Peak of Yuntai Mountain in Lianyungang 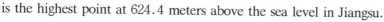 is the highest point at 624.4 meters above the sea level in Jiangsu.

河流 River

中国第一大河长江②流经江苏,经崇明岛泻入东海,在江苏省内流程 400 余公里。根据长江在江苏境内的流经区域和人文环境,江苏

② 长江:世界第三长河(仅次于尼罗河和亚马逊河),亚洲第一大河。全长 6 300 千米,发源于青海省,向东由上海注入中国。

The Yangtze River or Chang Jiang is the longest river in Asia. It's also the third-longest in the world, after the Nile in Africa and the Amazon in South America. The river is about 6,300 kilometers long and flows eastward from its source in Qinghai Province to the East China Sea at Shanghai.

又习惯性地分成苏南、苏北和苏中。

The Yangtze River, China's longest river, flows into Jiangsu and into the East China Sea around Chongming Island, with more than 400 kilometers in Jiangsu Province. According to the passing-through areas and cultural environment of the Yangtze River, Jiangsu is also usually divided into Southern Jiangsu, Northern Jiangsu and Central Jiangsu.

苏北地区包括徐州、连云港、宿迁、淮安、盐城五市。苏南地区包括南京、镇江、苏州、无锡、常州。苏中地区包括南通、泰州、扬州。

Northern Jiangsu include Xuzhou, Lianyungang, Suqian, Huai'an and Yancheng. Southern Jiangsu include Nanjing, Zhenjiang, Suzhou, Wuxi and Changzhou. Central Jiangsu areas include Nantong, Taizhou and Yangzhou.

淮河发源于河南,汇入黄海。江苏境内淮河属于下游,向南流入长江,成为长江支流之一。

The Huaihe River originates in Henan and flows into the Yellow Sea. The Huaihe River within Jiangsu belongs to the lower reaches and flows south to the Yangtze River.

③ 中国五大淡水湖包括:江西鄱阳湖,湖南洞庭湖,江苏太湖和洪泽湖,安徽巢湖。

The five freshwater lakes in China include Poyang Lake in Jiangxi, Dongting Lake in Hunan, Taihu Lake and Hongze Lake in Jiangsu, and Chaohu Lake in An'hui.

 六 湖泊 Lake

中国五大淡水湖③有两个位于江苏,太湖 2 250 平方公里,居第三;洪泽湖 2 069 平方公里,居第四。

Jiangsu has two of the five largest freshwater lakes in the country. Taihu Lake，2,250 square kilometers，ranks the third. Hongze Lake，2,069 square kilometers，ranks the fourth.

太湖横跨江苏、浙江两省，北临无锡，南濒湖州，西依宜兴，东近苏州。

Taihu Lake stretches through Jiangsu and Zhejiang Provinces，with Wuxi to the north，Huzhou to the south，Yixin to the west and Suzhou to the east.

洪泽湖位于淮安、宿迁两市境内。

Hongze Lake is located near the cities of Huai'an and Suqian.

行政区划 Administrative Division

截至2015年，江苏省共13个省属城市。

As of 2015，in Jiangsu Province，there are a total of 13 provincially administrated municipalities.

请说出江苏的13个省属城市的名称。

Please talk about the names of the thirteen cities in Jiangsu.

 人口 Population

　　2015 年,江苏常住人口达 7 900 万人,居中国第 5 位,占全国总人口 6%,是中国人口密度最大的省份。江苏绝大部分人口为汉族,占比 99.5%。

　　In 2015, Jiangsu had a permanent resident population of 79 million, with the largest population density and ranking the fifth most populous province in China. It accounts for 6% of the total national population. 99.5% of the population are Han people.

任务　Tasks

1. 单人活动　Individual Work

看图,请找出以下景点所在的城市。

Look at the pictures below and write down their locations.

2. 小组活动　Group Work

江苏名片:用你手中的相机记录你眼中的江苏名片,并作简要的介绍。

Jiangsu Card：Using photos you have taken，give a brief introduction of Jiangsu through your experiences.

第二章   历史述要
Chapter Two   Brief History

文化贴士2

江苏地域和古老的黄河流域一样,是中华民族诞生的摇篮之一。从远古时代起,在江苏这片土地上就有人类劳动、生息、繁衍,数十万年前南京一带就已经是人类聚居之地。**公元3—6世纪**①,先后有六个朝代在南京建都,南京成为中国南方的经济文化中心,十分繁华,留下了石头城、帝王陵墓与石刻等大量历史遗迹。**公元7—10世纪**②以后,京杭大运河贯通,隋朝统一中国,江苏成为富庶地区。全国经济重心南移,扬州成为当时全国最繁华的城市。**公元14—17世纪**③中叶以后,江苏的经济得到飞速发展,苏州、松江和南京等地成为中国资本主义萌芽的发祥地。南京和苏州是明代中国最大的两个丝织业中心。江苏正式建省始于清康熙六年(1667年),此后,江苏的经济、社会发展在中国一直名列前茅。

The area of Jiangsu is one of the cradles of modern China, just as the reaches of Yellow River. Since ancient times, there have been people living and farming. Hundreds of thousands of years ago, the area was inhabited by human beings. From the 3rd to 6th century A. D., dynasties began to repeatedly establish their capitals in Nanjing, and Nanjing became the economic and cultural center of the southern China. It was a great prosperous period which left behind lots of historical relics such as the Stone City, emperors' mausoleums and stone sculptures. From the 7th to 10th centuries A. D., the Grand Canal was dug. The Sui Dynasty unified ancient China and Jiangsu became an economic hub. Yangzhou became the country's most prosperous city due to moving the national economic center to the south of China. From the 14th to 17th centuries A. D., Jiangsu developed rapidly. Suzhou, Songjiang and Nanjing became the birthplace of China's capalist economy. Nanjing and Suzhou were the centers of the silk industry during the

① 公元3—6世纪,为三国、两晋、南北朝时期。

3—6th centuries A.D. were the Three Kingdoms, Jin Dynasty, Northern and Southern Dynasties.

② 公元7—10世纪,为唐、宋初。

7—10th centuries A. D. were the Tang and early Song Dynasties.

③ 公元14—17世纪,约为元明清时期。

14—17 centuries A. D. were the Yuan, Ming and Qing Dynasties.

Ming Dynasty. Jiangsu officially became a unified province in the Qing Dynasty in the sixth year of Emperor Kangxi's reign（1667）. Since then，Jiangsu has led the economic and social development in China.

表 1－1　中国朝代列表
Table 1－1　Table of Chinese Dynasties

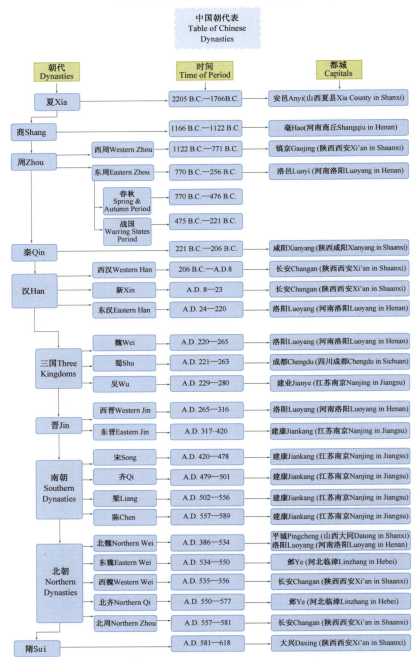

中国朝代表
Table of Chinese Dynasties

朝代 Dynasties		时间 Time of Period	都城 Capitals
夏Xia		2205 B.C.—1766B.C.	安邑Anyi(山西夏县Xia County in Shanxi)
商Shang		1166 B.C.—1122 B.C.	亳Hao(河南商丘Shangqiu in Henan)
周Zhou	西周Western Zhou	1122 B.C.—771 B.C.	镇京Gaojing (陕西西安Xi'an in Shaanxi)
	东周Eastern Zhou	770 B.C.—256 B.C.	洛邑Luoyi (河南洛阳Luoyang in Henan)
	春秋 Spring & Autumn Period	770 B.C.—476 B.C.	
	战国 Warring States Period	475 B.C.—221 B.C.	
秦Qin		221 B.C.—206 B.C.	咸阳Xianyang (陕西咸阳Xianyang in Shaanxi)
汉Han	西汉Western Han	206 B.C.—A.D.8	长安Changan (陕西西安Xi'an in Shaanxi)
	新Xin	A.D. 8—23	长安Changan (陕西西安Xi'an in Shaanxi)
	东汉Eastern Han	A.D. 24—220	洛阳Luoyang (河南洛阳Luoyang in Henan)
三国Three Kingdoms	魏Wei	A.D. 220—265	洛阳Luoyang (河南洛阳Luoyang in Henan)
	蜀Shu	A.D. 221—263	成都Chengdu (四川成都Chengdu in Sichuan)
	吴Wu	A.D. 229—280	建业Jianye (江苏南京Nanjing in Jiangsu)
晋Jin	西晋Western Jin	A.D. 265—316	洛阳Luoyang (河南洛阳Luoyang in Henan)
	东晋Eastern Jin	A.D. 317·420	建康Jiankang (江苏南京Nanjing in Jiangsu)
南朝 Southern Dynasties	宋Song	A.D. 420—478	建康Jiankang (江苏南京Nanjing in Jiangsu)
	齐Qi	A.D. 479—501	建康Jiankang (江苏南京Nanjing in Jiangsu)
	梁Liang	A.D. 502—556	建康Jiankang (江苏南京Nanjing in Jiangsu)
	陈Chen	A.D. 557—589	建康Jiankang (江苏南京Nanjing in Jiangsu)
北朝 Northern Dynasties	北魏Northern Wei	A.D. 386—534	平城Pingcheng (山西大同Datong in Shanxi) 洛阳Luoyang (河南洛阳Luoyang in Henan)
	东魏Eastern Wei	A.D. 534—550	邺Ye (河北临漳Linzhang in Hebei)
	西魏Western Wei	A.D. 535—556	长安Changan (陕西西安Xi'an in Shaanxi)
	北齐Northern Qi	A.D. 550—577	邺Ye (河北临漳Linzhang in Hebei)
	北周Northern Zhou	A.D. 557—581	长安Changan (陕西西安Xi'an in Shaanxi)
隋Sui		A.D. 581—618	大兴Daxing (陕西西安Xi'an in Shaanxi)

（continued）

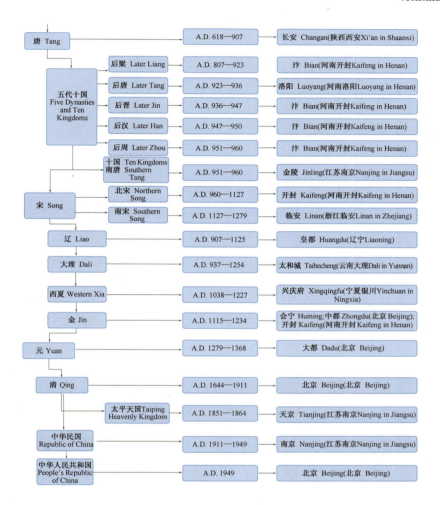

唐　Tang	A.D. 618—907	长安　Changan(陕西西安Xi'an in Shaanxi)
五代十国 Five Dynasties and Ten Kingdoms ─ 后梁　Later Liang	A.D. 807—923	汴　Bian(河南开封Kaifeng in Henan)
后唐　Later Tang	A.D. 923—936	洛阳　Luoyang(河南洛阳Luoyang in Henan)
后晋　Later Jin	A.D. 936—947	汴　Bian(河南开封Kaifeng in Henan)
后汉　Later Han	A.D. 947—950	汴　Bian(河南开封Kaifeng in Henan)
后周　Later Zhou	A.D. 951—960	汴　Bian(河南开封Kaifeng in Henan)
十国　Ten Kingdoms 南唐　Southern Tang	A.D. 951—960	金陵　Jinling(江苏南京Nanjing in Jiangsu)
宋　Song ─ 北宋　Northern Song	A.D. 960—1127	开封　Kaifeng(河南开封Kaifeng in Henan)
南宋　Southern Song	A.D. 1127—1279	临安　Linan(浙江临安Linan in Zhejiang)
辽　Liao	A.D. 907—1125	皇都　Huangdu(辽宁Liaoning)
大理　Dali	A.D. 937—1254	太和城　Taihecheng(云南大理Dali in Yunnan)
西夏　Western Xia	A.D. 1038—1227	兴庆府　Xingqingfu(宁夏银川Yinchuan in Ningxia)
金　Jin	A.D. 1115—1234	会宁　Huining;中都 Zhongdu(北京 Beijing);开封 Kaifeng(河南开封Kaifeng in Henan)
元　Yuan	A.D. 1279—1368	大都　Dadu(北京　Beijing)
清　Qing	A.D. 1644—1911	北京　Beijing(北京　Beijing)
太平天国Taiping Heavenly Kingdom	A.D. 1851—1864	天京　Tianjing(江苏南京Nanjing in Jiangsu)
中华民国 Republic of China	A.D. 1911—1949	南京　Nanjing(江苏南京Nanjing in Jiangsu)
中华人民共和国 People's Republic of China	A.D. 1949	北京　Beijing(北京　Beijing)

表 1－2 江苏历史发展简图
Table 1－2 Historical Development of Jiangsu

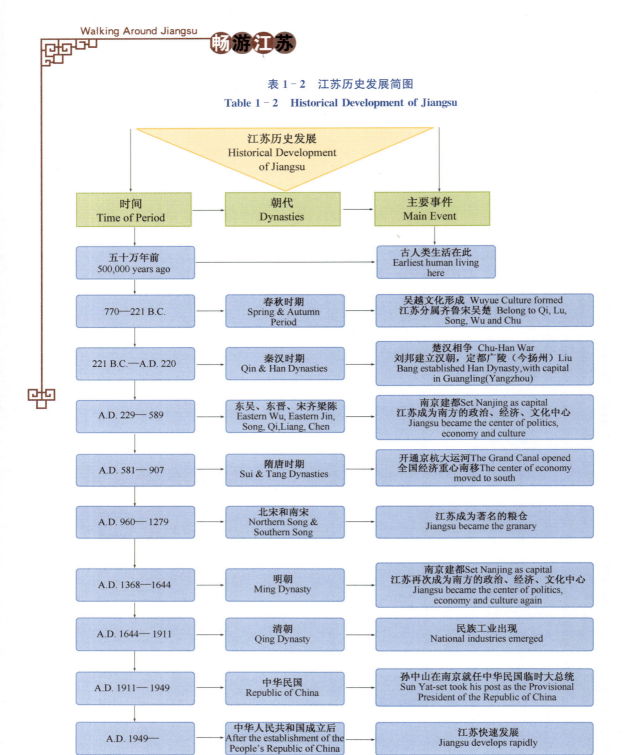

一 距今五十万年前 500,000 Years Ago

江苏是中华民族文明发源地之一。距今 50 万年前的南京汤山猿人，是迄今为止在江苏境内发现年代最早的古人类化石。

Jiangsu is one of the cradles of the Chinese civilization. Its earliest civilization can be traced back 500,000 years ago, with the excavation of the Tangshan Standing Human Fossil in Nanjing.

二 春秋时期 The Spring and Autumn Period

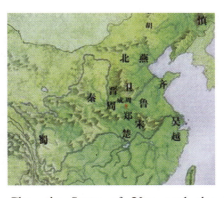

江苏在**春秋时期**④分属吴、楚、越、宋等国。江苏是吴越文化的发源地，也是长江流域文化的发源地。吴国开凿了中国最早的运河——邗沟，这是京杭大运河最早的一段航道。

In the Spring and Autumn Period，Jiangsu belonged to the State of Wu，the State of Chu，the State of Yue and the State of Song. Jiangsu is the birthplace of the ancient Wu and Yue culture as well as the Yangtze River culture. The State of Wu dug the earliest canal—Hangou，which also was the earliest section of Beijing-Hangzhou Canal.

④ 春秋时期是指公元前 770 年至公元前 476 年。

The Spring and Autumn Period refers to the years from 770 B.C. to 476 B.C.

三 秦汉时期 Qin and Han Dynasties

秦汉时期是江苏历史上最辉煌的时期之一。煮盐、纺织都有很大的进步,商业继续发展。

The period of Qin and Han Dynasties is one of the most magnificent periods in the history of Jiangsu. Industries like boiling salt from sea water and the textile developed quickly.

楚汉之争就发生在江苏。**刘邦**⑤是汉朝开国皇帝,是汉民族和汉文化的开拓者。**项羽**⑤,西楚霸王,与刘邦展开了历时四年的楚汉之争,最后兵败,于乌江自刎。

The War Between Chu and Han happened in Jiangsu. Liu Bang was the founding emperor of the Han Dynasty, pioneer of the Han ethnic group and Han culture. Xiang Yu, the king of the Western Chu, fought a four-year battle with Liu Bang, but in the end he was defeated and committed suicide in Wujiang.

⑤ 项羽和刘邦两位杰出人才,一位出生在江苏的宿迁,一位出生在江苏沛县。

Xiang Yu was born in Suqian, Jiangsu; Liu Bang was born in Peixian, Jiangsu.

四 三国时期 Three Kingdoms Period

三国⑥时期,苏南属吴,苏北归魏。南京当时为"建业",是吴国国都。之后,东晋时期,宋、齐、梁、陈四朝都选择南京为他们的国都,南京因此得名"六朝古都"。

During the Three Kingdoms Period, Southern Jiangsu belonged to the State of Wu, and Northern Jiangsu belonged to the State of Wei. Nanjing, named "Jianye" at that time, was the capital of the State of Wu. After that, during the Eastern Jin Dynasties of Song, Qi, Liang and Chen, each dynasty chose Nanjing as their capital. Therefore, Nanjing is well-known as the ancient capital of the six

⑥ 三国(220年—280年),是中国东汉与西晋之间的一段历史时期,指曹魏、蜀汉、东吴三个政权。

The Three Kingdoms (A. D. 220—280) is a long historical period, namely the reign of Wei, Shu and Wu.

dynasties.

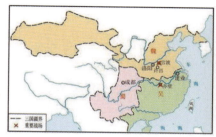 

五 隋唐时期 Sui and Tang Dynasties

京杭大运河于隋朝开通,江苏成为当时最富裕的地区。江苏是其主要流段,其中扬州受益最多,成为南北交通枢纽,物资流转中心。

In the Sui Dynasty, the Grand Canal opened. Jiangsu became the richest area in China at that time. Flow section in Jiangsu was the main access point, and Yangzhou benefited most from the Grand Canal. Yangzhou became the North-South transportation hub and the center of material transactions.

京杭大运河是中国也是世界上最长的古代运河。北起北京,南至杭州,流经北京、天津、河北、山东、江苏和浙江四省两市,贯通海河、黄河、淮河、长江、钱塘江五大水系,全长约 1 797 公里。

The Beijing-Hangzhou Grand Canal is the world's longest ancient canal. It runs from Beijing in the north to Hangzhou in the south. Running through Beijing，Tianjin，Hebei，Shandong，Jiangsu and Zhejiang，the Canal links five major river systems including Haihe River，Yellow River，Huaihe River，Yangtze River and Qiantang River，with a total length of about 1,797 kilometers.

六 明朝 Ming Dynasty

1368 年，朱元璋在南京建立明朝，并在此修建明孝陵，死后葬于此地。

In 1368, Emperor Zhu Yuanzhang established the Ming Dynasty in Nanjing. The Xiaoling Tomb of the Ming Dynasty was built and Emperor Zhu was buried there after his death.

明朝时期，江苏人口稠密，经济繁荣，纺织业和造船业发达。明成祖派郑和下西洋，成为航海史上空前壮举。

At the time, Jiangsu was densely populated and economically developed. The textile industry and ship-building industry were highly developed. Zheng He then set out to begin his voyage，which later became one of the greatest events in the world history.

南京是当时中国规模最大、人口最多的城市，也是全世界最大的城市。历时 27 年修建的南京明城墙是世界第一大城垣。

Nanjing was the largest city with largest population in China at that time，even the world. The Ming City Wall, built over 27 years，was the world's first big wall.

⑦ 张謇（1853 年 7 月 1 日—1926 年 8 月 24 日）江苏省海门市人，中国近代实业家、政治家、教育家，中国棉纺织领域早期的开拓者。

Zhang Jian （July 1, 1853—August 24, 1926）, was born in Haimen, Jiangsu Province. He was a famous Chinese industrialist, politician and educator, who was known as China's Cotton Textile Industry Pioneer.

七 清代 Qing Dynasty

清改南京辖区为江南省。清代时，正是江南丝织业的鼎盛时期。

During the Qing Dynasty, Nanjing was re-established as Jiangnan Province. The heyday of the Jiangnan silk industry happened just in the Qing Dynasty.

清末，工商业近代化的历史进程开启，先后涌现出南通张謇⑦、无

锡荣氏⑧等民族工业集团。

At the end of the Qing Dynasty, the historical modernization of industry and commerce came into being, and national industries emerged, such as Zhang Jian in Nantong and the Rongs in Wuxi.

⑧ 无锡荣氏是以荣毅仁为代表的中国民族资本家族,是新中国成立前著名的"面粉大王"、"棉纺大王"。

The Rongs, in Wuxi, was a Chinese family who invested in local enterprises. It was represented by Rong Yiren, who was the famous "Flour King" and "Cotton King" before the founding of the new China.

 民国时期 Republic of China

民国元年(1912 年),中华民国临时政府在南京成立,孙中山在此就任中华民国临时大总统。

In the first year of the Republic of China (1912), the provisional government of the Republic of China was established in Nanjing. Dr. Sun Yat-sen took office here as the Provisional President of the Republic of China.

国民党内战失败后,退至台湾,"中华民国中央政府"迁至台北市。

The Chinese Kuomingtang retreated to the island of Taiwan after being defeated in the Chinese Civil War, and the government of the Republic of China moved to Taipei, Taiwan (China).

 中华人民共和国 People's Republic of China

1949 年 4 月 23 日,南京解放。1949 年 6 月,江苏全境解放,1953 年成立江苏省,省会南京。

On April 23, 1949, Nanjing was liberated. In June 1949, Jiangsu was liberated completely. In 1953, Jiangsu Province was established with the provincial capital of Nanjing.

任务　Tasks

1. 单人活动　Individual Work

谈谈你所在国家或者省份的历史发展,与江苏的进行对比,看看各自的历史发展阶段有哪些大事件。

Talk about the historical development in your country or the province where you are, and then compare with Jiangsu, to see what big events happened in their respective histories.

2. 小组活动　Group Work

看图,将图片与文字相连,然后讨论每张图片的发生时期与历史事件。

Match the pictures with the description. Talk about the time and event which happened in each picture.

Site of the Treasure Boat Factory

Jiangning Imperial Silk Manufacturing Museum

Sunquan Tomb

The Grand Canal

The Xiaoling Tomb of the Ming Dynasty

Memorial Hall of the Victims in Nanjing Massacre by Japanese Invaders

☞ 文化贴士3

第三章　经济发展

Chapter Three　Economic Development

　　江苏位于长三角经济圈，该经济圈是中国第一大经济区，是中国中央政府定位的综合实力最强的经济中心、全球重要的先进制造业基地、中国率先跻身世界级城市群的地区。

　　江苏是中国近代工业的发祥地之一。依托该经济圈的发展优势，已经形成了门类齐全、具有相当规模的工业体系，并拥有一批骨干企业和名牌产品。江苏省综合经济实力在中国一直处于前列。江苏县域经济发达，2015 年，中国综合实力百强县市中，江苏占据17 席，并且包揽了前四名。2015 年，江苏省制造业总量继续保持全国第一；服务业占全省 GDP 比重 46.7%，超过制造业，成为主力军。江苏主动适应**新常态**①、全力推进转型升级，实现经济发展的新跨越。

Jiangsu is located on the Yangtze River Delta Economic Circle，which is the largest economic zone in China. It is an economic center with strongest overall power set by China's central government，as well as an important and advanced global manufacturing base. It is the first world-class city cluster in China.

Jiangsu is one of the birthplaces of China's modern industry. With the advantage of location，Jiangsu has developed a strong industrial system comprised of a number of famous enterprises and brand-name products. The comprehensive economic strength of Jiangsu Province has been on the top list in China. The county economy of Jiangsu is fully developed. By 2015，Jiangsu occupied 17 seats out of one-hundred cities and counties with strongest comprehensive power. The top four all come from Jiangsu. In 2015，the total production amount of Jiangsu's manufacturing industry continued to be the first. The service industry sped up and accounted for 46.7% of the provincial GDP，which has exceeded

① 新常态：习近平主席在 2014 年 5 月考察河南的行程中第一次提及"新常态"。

The New Normal Plan was first proposed by President Xi Jinping during his visit to Henan Provincein in May 2014.

the manufacturing industry and become the main force. Jiangsu is in the initiative to adapt to the New Normal, and spares no effort in promoting the transformation and upgrading to realize a new leap forward of economic development.

一 长三角经济圈 The Yangtze River Delta Economic Circle

② 长三角经济圈最初由 15 个城市组成,包括上海市,江苏省沿江的南京、苏州、无锡、常州、镇江、扬州、泰州、南通 8 市,浙江省的杭州、宁波、嘉兴、湖州、绍兴、舟山 6 市。

The Yangtze River Delta Economic Circle was originally composed of 15 cities, including Shanghai, 8 cities in Jiangsu （ Nanjing, Suzhou, Wuxi, Changzhou, Zhenjiang, Yangzhou, Taizhou and Nantong）, and 6 cities in Zhejiang （Hangzhou, Ningbo, Jiaxing, Huzhou, Shaoxing and Zhoushan）.

长三角经济圈② 是指以上海为中心,南京、杭州、合肥为副中心,包括江苏、浙江两省全境和安徽的合肥、淮南、滁州、芜湖、马鞍山等 30 个城市。在我国三大核心经济圈中,长三角是中国规模最大、实力最强、密度最高的经济圈。

The Yangtze River Delta Economic Circle is among China's three core economic circles. It is the economic circle with the largest scale, greatest strength and highest density. It comprises Shanghai as the center, Nanjing, Hangzhou and Hefei as deputy centers, including a total of 30 cities in Jiangsu and Zhejiang Provinces and Hefei, Huainan, Chuzhou, Wuhu, Maanshan, etc. in Anhui Province.

长三角经济圈临靠东海、黄海和长江,集"黄金海岸"和"黄金水道"于一身。

The Yangtze River Delta Economic Circle is located around the East China Sea, the Yellow Sea and the Yangtze River, with the "Gold Coast" and "Golden Waterway."

二 综合实力 Comprehensive Power

江苏综合经济实力位居中国大陆第二,仅次于广东省。

Jiangsu's comprehensive economic strength ranks second in China, only after Guangdong Province.

江苏是经济大省,以外向型经济为主,除引进外资外,江苏省的乡镇企业特别发达,形成了闻名于世的苏南模式。

Jiangsu is an economic power, based on export-oriented economy. Besides attracting foreign capital, Jiangsu Province focuses on township enterprises in particular, to form the world famous model of Sunan Economic Development.

三 区域发展 Regional Development

在苏锡常地区,城市工业区与小城镇沿着铁路、运河和高速公路发展,形成"交通走廊式"的城市分布格局。

In Suzhou, Wuxi and Changzhou, urban industrial areas and small towns develop along the railway, the canal and the highway, forming the urban distribution pattern of a "Transport Corridor."

江苏中国家纺城位于南通海门市,列全国布料及纺织品市场第三名。

China Home Textile City

is located in Haimen，Nantong City，which ranks the third in the national home textile market.

江苏丹阳眼镜城位于镇江丹阳市，是全国最大的眼镜批发市场。

Danyang Glass City is located in Danyang，Zhenjiang City，which is the country's largest wholesale glass market.

思考 Question

说说你知道的其他著名企业。

Talk about other name-brand enterprises you know.

四 江苏名企 Jiangsu Name-Brand Company

苏宁集团，创办于 1990 年，是中国民营企业 500 强，2014 年的综合收入和综合实力位居全国第一。

Suning Commerce Group Co.，Ltd，founded in 1990，is one of China's Top 500 private enterprises. In 2014，it ranked the first in the country for comprehensive income and comprehensive power.

徐工集团始建于 1989 年，是中国五百强企业之一，居世界工程机械行业第 5 位。

Xuzhou Construction Machinery Group Co.，founded in 1989，is one of the Top 500 enterprises in China，and ranks the fifth in machinery industry in the world.

任务　Tasks

1. 单人活动　Individual Work

请找一找中国的其他几个经济圈，并说说他们的经济发展特点。

Find out some other economic circles in China，and talk about their features of development.

序号 No.	名称 Name	城市 Location	特点 Feature
1			
2			
3			
...			

2. 小组活动 Group Work

采访你的中国朋友,讨论江苏省经济发展的动力因素有哪些,完成下表并进行汇报。

Interview your Chinese friends and discuss the reasons for economic development of Jiangsu Province in China. Fill out the following table and make a presentation.

因素 Factor	朋友 1 Friend 1	朋友 2 Friend 2	朋友 3 Friend 3	......
地理位置 Location				
政策 Policy				
其他 Others				

第四章　文化教育
Chapter Four　Culture and Education

☞ 文化贴士4

① 非物质文化遗产：江苏省的非物质文化遗产主要集中在文学、美术、音乐、舞蹈和戏曲。

Intangible Cultural Heritage in Jiangsu mainly focuses on literature, painting, music, dance and opera.

江苏以文化昌盛闻名全国，历代名人辈出，文化资源丰富，主要由"吴文化"、"金陵文化"、"淮扬文化"、"徐淮文化"等组成。江南以苏州为代表，是吴文化圈；江北以徐州为代表，语言和人文环境完全不同。江苏省**非物质文化遗产**①众多，江苏已有联合国教科文组织"人类非物质文化遗产代表作"10项，数量居中国第一。

江苏是教育大省，是中国首个实现县域义务教育发展基本均衡全覆盖省份，职业教育主要质量指标列全国第一，高等教育内涵建设主要指标在全国名列前茅。江苏实施留学江苏行动计划和茉莉花奖学金，2015年，全省外国留学生达2.6万人。

Jiangsu is famous for its prosperous culture, with famous celebrities and rich cultural resources, mainly composed by "Wu Culture," "Jinling Culture," "Huaiyang Culture" and "Xuhuai Culture." Suzhou represents southern Jiangsu culture, belonging to the Wu Cultural circle. Xuzhou represents northern Jiangsu culture with a totally different dialect and culture. Jiangsu owns plenty of intangible cultural heritage, with ten Intangible Cultural Heritage Representative Works entitled by UNESCO, the number ranking the first in China.

Jiangsu is a province of educational powerhouse. It strives to provide the best education in China, and provides all people with equal opportunities, power and hope. Jiangsu is the first province in China to realize the overall development of compulsory education. It ranks the first in quality education and vocational training. It comes out at the top list in China for higher education. Study in Jiangsu Project and Jasmine Jiangsu Government Scholarship are carried out. In 2015, there are 26,000 international students studying across the province.

表 1－3　中国教育体系框架图（简图）

Table 1－3　China's Education System Framework

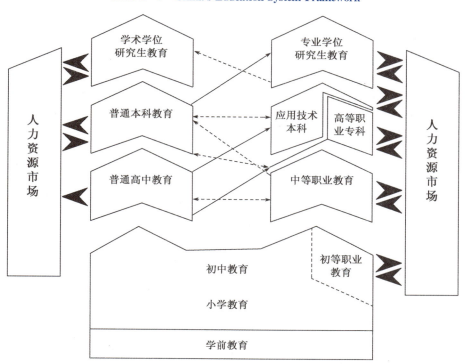

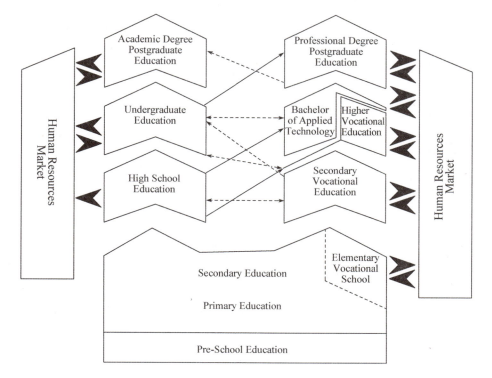

表 1-4 江苏教育体系框架图

Table 1-4 Jiangsu's Education System Framework

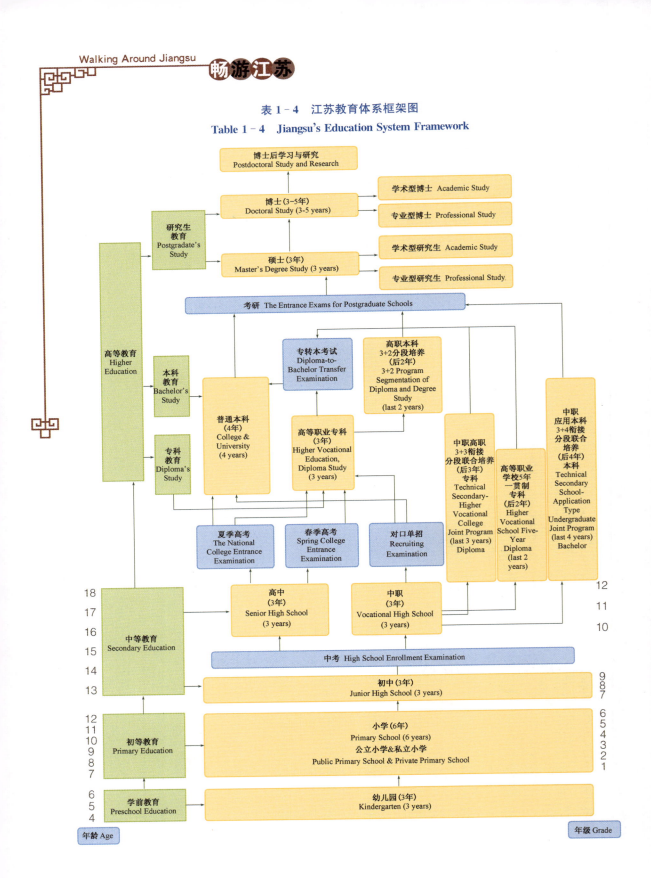

吴文化 Wu Culture

吴文化是中华文化的一个重要组成部分。3 100 多年前,吴在今苏州吴中区的木渎建都,逐步形成吴文化,是中国最具特色的区域。长期以来,被称作吴地的长江三角洲地区经济特别繁荣,其文化尤为发达,昆曲、评弹、苏绣等一批具有鲜明吴文化特色的优秀非物质文化遗产成为文化品牌。

Wu Culture is an important part of Chinese culture. Over 3,100 years ago, the Wu State established its capital in Mudu in Wuzhong District, Suzhou. Wu Culture gradually developed, and today this is the most notable characteristic of the region. The Yangtze River Delta Area, located in Wu State area, has long been part of the economic prosperity and developed culture. *Kunqu*, *Pingtan* and Suzhou Embroidery and other intangible cultural heritage have become the brand of Wu Culture.

 金陵文化 Jinling Culture

金陵文化,是以今南京为中心,辐射周边地区所形成的文化圈,是中华汉文明的重要组成部分。在地域上,金陵文化具有明显的吴文化特征;从历史上看,中国南北方文化交融,金陵文化也吸纳了中原主流文化的粗犷秩序,形成独树一帜的文化区域。金陵文化主要包括六朝文化、明文化和民国文化。

Jinling Culture, an important part of Chinese civilization, sets Nanjing as the center and also radiates into the surrounding areas. Jinling Culture absorbed the culture of Wu and Yue to develop distinctive characteristics. From history view, with a mix of southern and northern Chinese cultures, Jinling Culture also absorbed the mainstream culture of the Central Plains to form a unique regional culture. Jinling Culture includes Cultures of the Six Dynasties, the Ming Dynasty and the Republic of China.

 淮扬文化 Huaiyang Culture

淮扬文化的中心城市是国家历史文化名城扬州。淮扬地区河多水多,船多桥多,呈现出古、文、水、绿、秀的地域风貌,在南北文化交流

中形成清新优雅与豪迈超俊相结合的显性特征。扬剧、木偶戏、扬州漆器、扬州玉器等为世人所熟知。

Huaiyang Culture developed around Yangzhou, a historical and cultural city in China. There are lots of rivers, waters, bridges and ships. It displayed a complex geographical feature of history. It developed the typical feature being neat and fresh, generous and rough. Yangzhou Opera, Puppet Show, Yangzhou Lacquerware and Jade Ware are all well-known worldwide.

四 江苏教育 Jiangsu Education

近年来,随着江苏教育强省地位的不断加强,江苏致力于实现基础教育均衡发展、职业教育创新发展和高等教育高质量发展。目前,江苏教育的整体实力在中国领先,正接近中等发达国家水平。

Over recent years, with the aim of reinforcing Jiangsu's position as China's educational powerhouse, Jiangsu continues to strive to realize the balanced development of basic education, the innovative development of vocational training, and the quality development of higher education. Currently, Jiangsu education takes the lead in China and is approaching the standards of medium-developed countries.

表 1－5　江苏教育简况

Table 1－5　General Introduction of Jiangsu Education

Education Level	School Type	School Number	Student Number （min）	Percentage of Eligible Cohort
Pre-School (Elective)	Pre-School (3 yrs)	5,072	2.34	97.4
Grade 1—9 (Compulsory)	Primary (6 yrs)	4,034	4.71	100
	Junior High (3 yrs)	2,077	1.85	
Grade 10—12 (Elective)	Senior High (3 yrs)	567	1.03	99.9
	Vocational (3 yrs)	260	0.72	

(continued)

Education Level	School Type	School Number	Student Number (min)	Percentage of Eligible Cohort
Tertiary	Vocational (3 yrs)	83	0.68	51
	Universities and colleges (4—5 yrs)	51	1.01	
	Postgraduate (2—3 yrs)		0.15	
	Doctorate (3 yrs)			

义务教育 Compulsory Education

中国的义务教育年限为九年（小学六年，初中三年）。九年义务教育结束后，就读三年高中，学生参加高考，获取进入大学的资格。

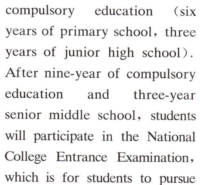

China adopts nine-year compulsory education （six years of primary school，three years of junior high school）. After nine-year of compulsory education and three-year senior middle school，students will participate in the National College Entrance Examination，which is for students to pursue higher education in China.

中考即"初中毕业和高中阶段招生考试"。考试科目主要有语文、数学、英语、物理、化学、政治、历史、地理、体育等科目，各地考试科目和考试时间均不一样。

The High School Enrollment Examination is a test for students graduating from junior high school to enter senior high school. The subjects mainly include Chinese，mathematics，English，physics，chemistry，politics，history，geography，sports，etc. The test subjects and test time vary from city to city.

高等教育 Higher Education

江苏是教育大省。截至 2015 年底，江苏有普通高等学校 162 所，在校生 187.1 万人，高校数和在校人数均居全国第一。根据美国汤森路透集团发布的数据，江苏有 21 所高校 81 个学科进入 ESI 全球前 1%，高校和学科数分列全国第一和第二。

Jiangsu Province focuses on education. By the end of 2015, there were 162 colleges and universities with 1.871 million students. The number of universities and on-campus students ranks the first in China. According to the data released by the United States' Townsend Reuters, 21 universities and 81 subjects in Jiangsu get into world top 1% of ESI (Essential Science Indicators), which rank the first and the second respectively in China.

南京大学、东南大学是全国知名的"985"大学。

Nanjing University and Southeast University are listed into Project 985.

表 1-6　江苏省 985、211 高校

Table 1-6　985 Project and 211 Project Universities

985 高校（2 所）Project 985
南京大学 Nanjing University
东南大学 Southeast University
211 高校（11 所）Poject 211
南京大学 Nanjing University 东南大学 Southeast University 苏州大学 Soochow University 河海大学 Hohai University 中国药科大学 China Pharmaceutical University 中国矿业大学（徐州）China University of Mining and Technology（Xuzhou Campus） 南京师范大学 Nanjing Normal University 南京理工大学 Nanjing University of Science and Technology 南京航空航天大学 Nanjing University of Aeronautics and Astronautics 江南大学 Jiangnan University 南京农业大学 Nanjing Agriculture University

国际教育 International Education

江苏地处中国对外开放的前沿，江苏的教育国际合作与交流也一直走在中国的前列。2015 年，江苏省共有 316 个由高等教育机构实

施的合作办学机构和项目，全球 4 大洲 12 个国家设立 29 个孔子学院和 20 个孔子课堂。

Located at the forefront of China's opening up to the world, Jiangsu's international cooperation and exchange have always been a main priority. By 2015, there were 316 joint institutions and programs implemented by higher educational institutes in Jiangsu Province. There are 29 Confucius Institutes and 20 Confucius Classrooms overseas in 12 countries of 4 continents.

文化遗产 Cultural Heritage

江苏有苏州园林、明孝陵、中国大运河等世界文化遗产和昆曲、雕版印刷技艺、扬州剪纸等世界非物质文化遗产。

Jiangsu has Suzhou Garden, Xiaoling Tomb of the Ming Dynasty, the Grand Canal of China and other world cultural heritage, such as *Kunqu*, engraving, Yangzhou paper-cutting and other world intangible cultural heritage.

江苏省官方语言是现代汉语普通话。历史上主要有三种官话。南京话（Nankinese）在历史上长期是中国的官方语言。江淮官话主要在扬州、盐城、淮安使用。吴方言主要是苏锡常

思考 Question

找找江苏还有哪些文化遗产。

Find the cultural heritage in Jiangsu Province.

地区使用,苏州话是吴语的代表方言之一。

The official language of Jiangsu Province is mandarin. There are mainly three kinds of Mandarin Chinese in history. Historically, Nanjing dialect（Nankinese）was China's official language，while Jianghuai Mandarin is mainly spoken in Yangzhou，Yancheng and Huai'an. Wu dialect is mainly spoken in Suzhou，Wuxi and Changzhou. Suzhou is one of the representatives of Wu dialect.

六 文化活动 Cultural Activity

中国南京国际梅花节
China International Plum Blossom Festival

② 中国四大梅园包括南京梅花山梅园、武汉东湖磨山梅园、无锡梅园和上海淀山湖梅园。

The four plum gardens in China refer to Plum Hill in Nanjing, Donghu Moshan Mountain in Wuhan, Plum Garden in Wuxi and Dingshanhu Plum Garden in Shanghai.

每年2月最后一个星期六至3月18日在南京钟山风景区梅花山举办。梅花山的梅园是**中国四大梅园**②之一。

From the last Saturday of February to March 18, the Chinese International Plum Blossom Festival is held in Nanjing on Plum Blossom Hill, which is one of four Plum Blossom Gardens in China.

溱潼会船节
Qintong Boat Festival

每年清明次日在泰州姜堰区溱潼镇举行富有民俗特色的溱潼会船节。

On the second day of Tomb-Sweeping Day，Qintong Boat Festival is held in Qintong Town of Jiangyan District，Taizhou City.

任务　Tasks

1. 单人活动　Individual Work

请将以下图片与相对应的文字连线。

Match pictures with words.

漆器
Lacquerware

剪纸
Paper-Cutting

泥人
Clay Figure

紫砂壶
Clay Pot

2. 小组活动　Group Work

采访你的中国朋友，找找江苏还有哪些民俗文化节完成下表并进行汇报。

Interview your Chinese friends and find out other cultural festivals in Jiangsu. Fill out the following table and make a presentation.

民俗文化节 Name	朋友1 Friend 1	朋友2 Friend 2	朋友3 Friend 3	……

第二篇　江苏城市
Part Two　Cities in Jiangsu Province

第一章　南京市
Chapter One　Nanjing City

① 十朝都会：东吴，东晋，南朝的宋、齐、梁、陈，南唐，明，太平天国以及国民党政府建都于此。

The capital of the Ten Regimes: East Wu; East Jin; Song, Qi, Liang and Chen of Southern Dynasties; South Tang; Ming; the Taiping Heavenly Kingdom and the Kuomintang Government.

南京，简称宁，有"金陵"、"建康"、"石头城"之称，是江苏省会，地处中国东部地区，长江下游。全市下辖 11 个区，总面积 6 597 平方公里，常住人口 821.61 万（2014 年）。

南京拥有 6 000 多年文明史、近 2 600 年建城史和近 500 年的建都史，是中国四大古都之一，素有"六朝古都"、"**十朝都会**"①之美誉。南京历史源远流长，文化底蕴厚重，各类遗存众多，是中华文明的重要发祥地之一，是黄河文明与长江文明的交汇地。

南京的文化，是传统和现代的统一。汤山的猿人化石把南京的史前痕迹前溯了 50 万年。名列世界文化遗产的明孝陵，得到精心保护的南朝石刻、南唐二陵和明城墙，独特历史地位的中山陵、总统府及众多民国建筑，享誉中华的第一商圈新街口，地标性建筑紫峰大厦，现代都市生活 1912 街区，将南京的历史与现代完美结合。

本章主要从南京的历史与文化教育两个角度去展示南京这个文化之都、博爱之都和绿色之都。

Nanjing（short for Ning），also called Jinling, Jiankang and the Stone City, is the capital of Jiangsu Province in East China. Running through the city are lower reaches of the Yangtze River. The city has 11 districts with a total area of 6,597 square kilometers，and a population of 8,216,100 permanent residents（2014）.

Nanjing enjoys a history of over 6,000 years. The city itself was founded 2,500 years ago and spent about 500 years as capitals for various dynasties. As one of the four ancient capitals, Nanjing, the Capital of Six Ancient Dynasties and the Capital of Ten Regimes, is a vital cradle of Chinese civilization and over a long stretch of time. It has been the political and cultural pivot of China, with rich cultural heritage and historical relics.

Nanjing culture is full of classics and modernity. Tangshan Ape-man Fossils trace prehistory of Nanjing back to 500,000 years ago. Xiaoling Tomb of the Ming Dynasty, on the list of world cultural heritage, is well-protected Stone Sculptures and Mausoleums of the Southern Dynasties. There are two Mausoleums of the Southern Tang and the Ming City Wall, as well as Sun Yat-sen's Mausoleum with a unique historical position. In the downtown area, one can find the Presidential Palace and the building of the Republic of China, famous business circle of Xinjiekou, the Zifeng Tower (the land mark of Nanjing), the 1912 blocks for modern urban life.

This chapter presents Nanjing from historical and cultural aspects, to display a City of Culture, a City of Fraternity and a City of Greenery.

第一节　古都文化

Unit One　Culture of the Ancient City

① 明宝船遗址：
宝船是郑和船队中最
大的海船，主要建造
于南京宝船厂。

Ming Treasure
Boat Sites: the
Treasure Ship is the
largest in Zhenghe's
team, which was
mainly built by Nanjing
Ship Company.

文化资源是南京市最具吸引力的核心之一。南京是国家级历史文化名城，见证了中国近现代荣辱兴衰的历史。

南京是六朝古都，十朝都会，六朝文化、明文化、民国文化在历史上留下了深刻的时代烙印。六朝时期是中华民族大迁徙、大融合的时代，各种思想和民族文化的激荡让这一时期的文化有着特殊的魅力。南京是明文化和民国文化的发源地与核心区域。明朝在南京定都而开创的明文化，代表了中国历史文化发展的又一高峰。它在都城文化、建筑文化、中外文化交流等方面都有非凡的创举，拥有明孝陵、明故宫、明城墙、**明宝船遗址**①等一大批重要文化遗存。南京拥有得天独厚的民国历史文化资源，是我国民国文化遗存最多的城市。中山陵、灵谷寺、总统府等民国建筑在中国近代史上有着独特的地位。

Cultural resources are one of the most attractive parts of Nanjing, which is known for a famous historical and cultural city. It has witnessed the rise and fall of modern Chinese history.

Nanjing was the capital of Six Ancient Dynasties and the Capital of Ten Regimes. The culture of the Six Ancient Dynasties, the Ming Dynasty and Republic of China left a deep imprint on China's history. It was a period of Chinese great migration and national amalgamation, which enabled the growth of thought and cultural progress. Nanjing is the cradle and the center of the Ming Culture and the Culture of the Republic of China. Ming Culture was established during the Ming Dynasty in Nanjing, which represented a peak in the development of Chinese history and culture. Its capital culture, construction and Sino-foreign cultural exchanges were unique in the world. Xiaoling Tomb of the Ming Dynasty, Ming Palace, Ming City Wall and Ming Treasure Boat Sites are important cultural relics left from that time. Nanjing also has unique historical and cultural resources of the modern Republic of China, with the most popular cultural heritage of the Republic of China. Sun Yat-sen's Mausoleum, Linggu Temple and the Presidential Palace all play a unique role in the history of Chinese modern history.

 ## 六朝文化 The Culture of the Six Ancient Dynasties

Museum of the Six Dynasties

Ming City Wall

六朝②承汉启唐，创造了极其辉煌灿烂的"六朝文明"，在科技、文学、艺术等诸方面均达到了空前的繁荣，开创了中华文明新的历史纪元。

The Six Dynasties serve as a connection between the Han Dynasty and the Tang Dynasty, creating the splendid "Civilization of Six Dynasties." During this time, Nanjing reached an unprecedented prosperity in science and technology, literature and art, entering a new era of Chinese civilization.

这六个朝代都建都于南京（古称建康）。六朝时期的南京城是世界上第一个人口超过百万的城市，和古罗马城并称为"世界古典文明两大中心"。

The Six Dynasties all established their capitals in Nanjing (Jiankang at that time). Nanjing was the first city in the world with over 1 million of population. It is well-known as one of the "two centers of the world classical civilization" with the ancient city of Rome.

作为六朝古都，南京拥有丰富的六朝文化资源，如六朝祭坛、孙权

② 六朝是指中国历史上三国至隋朝期间，东吴、东晋、宋、齐、梁、陈这六个朝代。

The Six Dynasties include East Wu, East Jin, Song, Qi, Liang and Chen from the period of the Three Kingdoms to the Sui Dynasty.

By Wang Xizhi

Tomb of Sun Quan

墓、石头城等,还有王羲之、顾恺之、谢灵运等名家大师的遗迹和名篇。

As the ancient capital of the Six Dynasties,Nanjing has rich cultural resources including the Altar, Sun Quan's Tomb, the Stone City, famous relics and masterpieces by Wang Xizhi, Gu Kaizhi, Xie Lingyun, etc.

孙权是葬于钟山的第一位帝王,开启了以后历代在南京定都的帝王或政治家喜爱以钟山作为陵址的先河。

Emperor Sun Quan was the first emperor buried in the Purple Mountain,which started selecting Purple Mountain by famous emperors and politicians as their tomb sites.

二 明文化之明孝陵
Ming Culture—Xiaoling Tomb of the Ming Dynasty

③朱元璋(1328—1398),是明朝开国皇帝,建立了明朝。

Emperor Zhu Yuanzhang was the founding emperor of the Ming Dynasty.

思考 Question

为什么取名明孝陵呢?"孝"什么意思呢?

Why is it called Xiaoling Tomb of the Ming Dynasty? What does Xiao mean?

Xiaoling Tomb of the Ming Dynasty

明孝陵位于南京市东郊紫金山(钟山)南面,是明朝开国皇帝**朱元璋**③与马皇后的陵墓,已被列入《世界文化遗产名录》。明孝陵建于 1381 年,历时 17 年时间建成,至今已有 600 多年的历史,是我国现存古代最大的帝王陵之一。

Xiaoling Tomb of the Ming Dynasty lies below the southern peak of the Purple Mountain in Nanjing, which is the burial place of Emperor Zhu Yuanzhang, the founder of the Ming Dynasty, and his queen. It has been listed into a World Cultural Heritage. Xiaoling Tomb of the Ming Dynasty was built in 1381 and took over 17 years to complete. It is one of the largest

Golden Water Bridge

Main Entrance

Sacred Way

Square City

existing emperor's mausoleums in Chinese history.

明孝陵是中国明陵之首,代表了明初建筑和石刻艺术的最高成就,直接影响了明清两代500多年帝王陵寝的形制,在中国帝陵发展史上有着特殊的地位,故而有"明清皇家第一陵"的美誉。

The Xiaoling Tomb of the Ming Dynasty is the first Chinese Ming Tomb, representing the highest achievement of the early Ming Dynasty architecture and stone carving art. It has a direct impact on the Emperor Mausoleum shape for the next 500 years in the Ming and Qing Dynasties. It has a special status in the history of the development of Chinese mausoleums, which earns the reputation of "the first royal mausoleum of the Ming and Qing Dynasties."

陵墓分为两部分:第一部分是陵墓神道,包括下马坊、大金门、神功圣德碑及碑亭(俗称四方城)、神道和御河桥。第二部分是明孝陵寝主体建筑,包括文武方门(即正门)、碑殿、享殿、明楼和宝顶等。

The Xiaoling Tomb of the Ming Dynasty is divided into two parts: the first part is where the tomb starts from the Dismounting-from-Horse Archway, the Square City, finally guiding the way to the Sacred Way and Golden Water Bridge. The second part is composed of the Main Entrance, Tablet Pavilion, Xiaoling Palace, the Citadel of Treasures and Tomb Mound.

三 明文化之夫子庙和秦淮风光
Ming Culture—Confucius Temple & Qinhuai River Scenic Area

Confucius Temple

Qinhuai River

Confucius Temple

Screen Wall

秦淮河,全长110千米,是南京的母亲河。自六朝至明清,十里秦淮的繁华景象和特有的风貌被历代文人所讴歌。

Qinhuai River, with a total length of 110 kilometers, is the "Mother River" of Nanjing. From the Six Dynasties to the Ming and Qing Dynasties, prosperity and innovation of Qinhuai River were praised by scholars.

闻名海内外的夫子庙是秦淮风光带的核心游览部分,是首个免费对公众开放的国家5A级旅游景区。夫子庙首建于宋代1034年。

The Confucius Temple, which is the most lively place at inner Qinhuai River, is the first 5A scenic attraction opened to the public for free. It was originally constructed in 1034 during the Song Dynasty.

夫子庙是供奉和祭祀**孔子**④的地方,中国四大文庙之一,是明清时期南京的文教中心。

The Confucius Temple is one of the four largest Confucian Temples in China. People went there to worship

④ 孔子(公元前551年—公元前479):是中国古代儒家学派的创始人。

Confucius (551—479 B. C.): the founder of the philosophy of Confucianism in ancient Chinese history.

Jiangnan Examination Hall

The Lantern Festival

Confucius, and it was also the cultural and educational center of Nanjing in the Ming and Qing Dynasties.

照壁，建于明万历三年（公元 1575 年），长 110 米，高 10 米，是全国最大的照壁。

The Screen Wall, built in Ming Wanli's third year of reign（A.D. 1575），is 110 meters long and 10 meters high，and ranks top among all the screen walls across the country.

江南贡院是夫子庙地区三大古建筑群之一。其规模之大、占地之广居全国各省贡院之冠，是中国古代最大**科举**⑤考场。

Jiangnan Examination Hall is one of the three ancient buildings in the Confucius Temple area. It is the largest Chinese ancient imperial examination hall for its size and the area.

⑤ 科举：是中国古代通过考试选拔官吏的制度。

The Civil Service Examination System is for the ancient Chinese government to select officials through imperial examination.

四 民国文化之中山陵
Culture of the Republic of China—Sun Yat-sen's Mausoleum

Dr. Sun Yat-sen's Mausoleum

中山陵是**孙中山**⑥先生的陵墓，位于南京市东郊钟山风景名胜区内，从空中往下看，像一座平躺在绿色毯子上的"自由钟"，被誉为"中国近代建筑史上第一陵"。

Dr. Sun Yat-sen's Mausoleum is located in the Purple Mountain Scenic Area in the eastern suburb of Nanjing City，Jiangsu Province. The whole scenic area represents a bell as seen from the air，which is known as the "First Mausoleum of China Modern Architecture."

⑥ 孙中山（1866—1925），又名孙文、孙逸仙，是中国近代民主主义革命的开拓者，中华民国和中国国民党缔造者，三民主义的倡导者。

Sun Zhongshan (also named Sun Yat-sen and Sun Wen, 1866—1925) was a Chinese revolutionary and political leader, often referred to as the "Father of Modern China," the founder of the Republic of China and Chinese Kuomintang, and a promoter of the "Three Principles of Peoples."

中山陵 1926 年春动工,至 1929 年夏建成。主要建筑有博爱坊、墓道、陵门、石阶、碑亭、祭堂和墓室等,排列在一条中轴线上,体现了中国传统建筑"天人合一"的风格。

Fraternity Archway

The majestic mausoleum's construction was started in the spring of 1926 and completed in the summer of 1929. It consists of the Fraternity Archway, Tomb Avenue, layers of steps, the Tablet Pavilion, the Memorial Hall and the Coffin Chamber. It ascends gradually along with the mountain, with the central axis line running from south to north, reflecting the traditional style of China's architecture and the theory that "harmony between human and nature".

Tomb Avenue

陵墓入口处有高大的花岗石牌坊,上有中山先生手书的"博爱"两个金字,陵门上方刻有"天下为公"四个金字。

At the entrance of the Mausoleum, an archway was built with "BOAI," which means "fraternity" in English. Above the archway, Chinese characters meaning "the whole world as one community" were engraved.

Memorial Hall

Music Platform

纪念堂有孙中山先生大理石坐像,高 4.6 米,是世界著名雕刻家的杰作。

Dr. Sun Yat-sen's memorial hall has a marble sitting figure,

4.6 meters high，which is a world famous sculptor's masterpiece.

五 民国文化之总统府 Culture of the Republic of China— Presidential Palace

Presidential Palace

Zichao Tower

Xuyuan Garden

Unmoored Stone-Boat

总统府已有 600 多年的历史，最早建于明代初期，是保存完好的近代中西建筑遗迹。总统府历史文化氛围浓厚，存有珍贵的文物和史料，风景优美。

The Presidential Palace, with more than 600 years of history，was founded in the early Ming Dynasty. The Presidential Palace is well preserved，as the modern Chinese and Western architectural remains. It has a unique and profound historical and cultural atmosphere，precious cultural relics and historical materials，and beautiful scenery.

总统府既有中国古代传统的江南园林，也有近代西风东渐时期的建筑遗存，是南京民国建筑的主要代表。

The Presidential Palace has ancient Chinese Jiangnan garden and the remains of modern western architecture. It is the representative building of the Republic of China.

总统府，明朝初年曾为归德侯府和汉王府，清朝为两江总督署，太平天国占领南京后，在此建立天王府。

The Presidential Palace served as the Marquise Guide's

Office of Provisional President

Residence and then Prince Han's Residence in the early years of the Ming Dynasty. Later，it also served as the official residences of Liangjiang Viceroy's in the Qing Dynasty，and the Heavenly King's Palace in the period of the Taiping Heavenly Kingdom after Hong Xiuquan occupied Nanjing.

南京总统府自近代以来,多次成为中国政治军事的中枢、重大事件的策源地。1912 年 1 月 1 日,孙中山先生在此宣誓就任中华民国临时大总统。

The Presidential Palace became the center of political and military events in modern China. On January 1st，1912，Dr. Sun Yat-sen was sworn here as the Provisional President of the Republic of China and made it his office.

任务　Tasks

1. 单人活动　Individual Work

看图说话:南京明文化遗迹众多,观察以下图片,搜索相关资源,说说图片上的景物。

Look at the pictures，search the Internet and talk about the following pictures of cultural relics of the Ming Dynasty.

朝天宫 Chaotian Palace

中华门 Zhonghua Gate

孝陵 Xiaoling Tomb of the Ming Dynasty

明城墙 Ming City Wall

2. 小组活动　Group Work

请点击"夫子庙秦淮河风光带"官网 http：//www.njfzm.net/，按照"虚拟旅游"结合本景区图，设计自己的游览线路。

Please click http：//www.njfzm.net/ to see the following map and design your own tourism route.

3. 单人活动　Individual Work

南京的民国建筑遗迹众多，请登录南京旅游信息 http：//www.nju.gov.cn/，查看南京还有哪些民国建筑？你最喜欢哪个？

There is a lot of Republican-Era Architecture in Nanjing. Log onto the Welcome to Nanjing Tourism，http：//www.nju.gov.cn/web to check out other architecture，then talk about which one do you like most.

提示(Clues)：

南京的民国建筑既有北方建筑的粗犷，南方建筑的细腻，又融合了西方建筑的典雅，现代建筑的简洁明快。

Republican-Era Architecture in Nanjing combines the simple character of buildings from the North，the delicate character of buildings in the South，and also the elegance of western architecture with the simplicity and brightness of modern architecture.

第二节　书香文化

Unit Two　Culture of Literary

　　南京自古就是一座崇文重教的城市,有"天下文枢"、"东南第一学"的美誉。南京历来重视对历史文化的传承和弘扬,南京建有众多博物馆,包括南京博物院、南京市博物馆(朝天宫)、南京市民俗博物馆(甘熙故居)、南京六朝博物馆、云锦博物馆、江宁织造博物馆等,以及近些年越来越多的公共阅读空间如先锋书店的兴起,形成了南京重视人文、看重阅读的书香文化氛围。

　　南京是中国高等教育资源最集中的五大城市之一,国家三大高等教育中心,国家四大科研教育中心,科教综合实力仅次于北京、上海①。南京共有三个大学城,分别是位于栖霞区的仙林大学城、江宁区的江宁大学城和浦口区的浦口大学城。

① 截至 2015 年,南京共有高等院校 44 所,其中 985 高校 2 所、211 高校 8 所,仅次于北京和上海。

Until 2015, Nanjing has a total of 44 colleges and universities. Among them there are two "985" and eight "211" universities, ranking third only after Beijing and Shanghai.

Nanjing is a city that has put a great emphasis on academic education since ancient times, with the reputation of "the Gateway of All Scholars" and the "No. 1 Academy in Southeast." Nanjing has always paid much attention to carrying forward their historical and cultural heritage. There are numerous museums, including the Nanjing Museum, Nanjing Municipal Museum (Chaotian Palace), Nanjing Folk Museum (Gan's Grand Courtyard), Nanjing Museum of Six Dynasties, Nanjing Yunjin Museum, and Jiangning Weaving Museum. Recently, Nanjing has begun to focus on public reading spaces, such as Xianfeng Bookstore, which is placing a renewed emphasis on the cultural merits of reading.

Nanjing is one of five big cities concentrating China's higher educational resources. It is one of three national top higher education centers, as well as one of four big scientific research and education centers. The scientific and educational comprehensive power of Nanjing ranks the third only after Beijing and Shanghai. There are three main university centers: Nanjing Xianlin University Center located in Qixia District, Jiangning University

Center located in Jiangning District，and Pukou University Center located in Pukou District.

 南京博物院 **Nanjing Museum**

The Gate of Nanjing Museum

Nanjing Museum

南京博物院② 是我国最早创建的博物馆之一。南京博物院的前身国立中央博物院是 1933 年由我国近代教育家蔡元培先生倡议创建的。

Nanjing Museum is the earliest museum in China, built in 1933 as the National Central Museum which was founded by Mr. Cai Yuanpei, a very famous educator in Chinese history.

南京博物院是仅次于中国国家博物馆的中国第二大博物馆，是中国三大博物馆之一，是一座大型综合性的省级历史与艺术类博物馆，共设历史馆、特展馆、数字馆、艺术馆、民国馆、非遗馆六馆。

Nanjing Museum is the second largest museum after the National Museum of China. It is one of the three national museums, a large comprehensive provincial history and art museum. It has six exhibition halls: the History Hall, the Special Exhibition Hall, the Digital Hall, the Art Hall, the Hall of the Republic of China, and the Intangible Cultural Heritage Hall.

南京博物院的建筑设计思想力图体现中国早期的建筑风格，是一座仿辽式建筑。现有各类藏品 42 万件，国宝级文物和国家一级文物有两千件以上。馆藏文物的年代跨度较大，而且各类文物的划分也比较细致，包括珍宝、玉器、明清瓷器、织绣等。

② 南京博物院是中国的三大博物馆之一，其他两座分别是北京故宫博物院和台北故宫博物院。

Nanjing Museum is one of the three national museums in China. The other two are the Palace Museum in Beijing and Taipei Museum in Taipei.

Mingguo Style Street

The architectural design of Nanjing Museum tries to reflect the architectural style of early Chinese buildings, in an imitation of Liao style building. It has a collection of 420,000 pieces of relics, more than 2,000 pieces of which are of national treasures. There are all kinds of artifacts, including treasure, jade, porcelain from the Ming and Qing Dynasties, embroidery, weave and so on.

南京以"民国"为特色,民国馆特别受游客的欢迎。

Nanjing is featured with the "Republic of China," so the Republic of China Hall is particularly popular with tourists.

二 南京著名学府 Famous Universities in Nanjing

南京是我国科教第三城,拥有众多高校,如南京大学、东南大学、南京师范大学、中国药科大学等。这些高校历史悠久,时至今日,还保留着当年的建筑风格。

Nanjing is the third-largest city by science and education in China, with a large number of colleges and universities, such as Nanjing University, Southeast University, Nanjing Normal University and China Pharmaceutical University. These colleges and universities have a long history, retaining the architectural style of the year they were built.

③ 南京大学有鼓楼、浦口、仙林三个校区。

Nanjing University consists of three campuses, Gulou, Pukou and Xianlin.

Nanjing University

南京大学③是中国首批"985 工程"和"211 工程"重点建设高校,是中国常青藤盟校——C9 成员之一,也是"珠峰计划"首批 11 所名校之一,为中国著名学府。

Nanjing University（NJU）

is one of the oldest and most prestigious institutions of higher education in China，belonging to Project 985 and Project 211. It is one of the members of the ivy league C9 in China，and one out of eleven famous universities of the Mount Everest Project.

南京大学历史悠久，其前身可追溯到孙吴永安元年的南京太学。南京大学的名称、建筑也发生着变化，但依然保留着北大楼、小礼堂等建筑，以及孙中山、约翰拉贝、赛珍珠等名人故居，是我国大学中不可多得的人文景观荟萃之地，被誉为"中国最温和的大学"。1986 年，南京大学和美国约翰斯·霍普金斯大学共同创办南京大学—约翰·霍普金斯大学中美文化研究中心，是国际知名的跨国教学与研究机构，是中美两国高等教育国际合作的典范。

Nanjing University has a long history，which can be traced back to the Imperial College of Nanjing from the first year of the Wu State. The names and buildings of Nanjing University have changed，but there are still some buildings kept such as the North Building，Small Chapel and former residences of Sun Yat-sen，John Rabe，Pearl S. Buck and other celebrities. NJU is a unique place with many human landscapes，known as "China's Most Gentle University."

In 1986，the Johns Hopkins University—Nanjing University Center for Chinese and American Studies was established. It is a famous international teaching and research institution，which has become a model of international cooperation in higher education between China and the United States.

Southeast University

东南大学是中央直管、教育部直属的全国重点大学，是"985 工程"和"211 工程"重点建设的大学之一，素有"学府圣地"和"东南学府第一流"之美誉。

Southeast University（SEU）

④ 东南大学建有四牌楼、九龙湖、丁家桥等校区。
Southeast University consists of three campuses：Sipailou，Jiulonghu and Dingjiaqiao.

is one of the key national universities administered directly under the Central Government and the Ministry of Education of China. It is also one of the universities of Project 211 and Project 985 to be built up as a world-class university. It is known as an "Institution of Learning" and a "Top University in the Southeast."

东南大学有 5 个国家一级重点学科。在 2012 年第三轮全国学科评估中，生物医学工程、交通运输工程、艺术学理论 3 个学科位列全国第一位，排名第一的学科数并列全国高校第七位。

SEU has 5 national key disciplines. In the third round of the Chinese Discipline Ranking in 2012, the three disciplines of bio-medical engineering, communication and transportation engineering as well as art theory rank the first nationwide, occupying the seventh place in terms of the number.

Nanjing Normal University

南京师范大学是国家"211工程"重点建设的江苏省属重点大学。其前身可追溯到 1902 年创办的三江师范学堂，该学堂是中国高等师范教育的发祥地之一。南京师范大学拥有仙林、随园、紫金三个校区，随园校区有

着"东方最美丽的校园"之美誉。

Nanjing Normal University（NNU）is a "Project 211" university administered under Jiangsu Province. The history of NNU can be traced back to Sanjiang Normal Institute in 1902，which was the birthplace of China's higher education for teachers. NNU consists of three campuses including Xianlin，Suiyuan and Zijin. Suiyuan has a reputation as "the Most Beautiful Campus in the East."

任务   Tasks

1. 文化体验活动   Hands-on Work

四人一组，参观南京博物院，调查南京博物院六个展览馆内的特色藏品。

Work in groups of four to visit and investigate the special relics of each hall of Nanjing Museum.

艺术馆 Art Hall

数字馆 Digital Hall

民国馆 Hall of the Republic of China

历史馆 History Hall

特展馆 Special Exhibition Hall

非遗馆 Intangible Cultural Heritage Hall

2. 小组活动　Group Work

点击以下南京著名学府的网站链接，了解相关信息，完成下表任务，将列表中的信息与图片连起来。

Search the Internet and find out more information on well-known universities in Nanjing，then match the following information in each table with the logo.

- 南京中医药大学 Nanjing University of Chinese Medicine
  http：//www. njutcm. edu. cn/
- 南京师范大学 Nanjing Normal University
  http：//www. njnu. edu. cn/

- 南京大学 Nanjing University
  http://www.nju.edu.cn/
- 南京理工大学 Nanjing University of Science & Technology
  http://www.njust.edu.cn/

前身为三江师范学堂,有着"东方最美丽的校园"之美誉,拥有仙林、随园、紫金三个校区。

It can be traced back to Sanjiang Normal Institute, and known as the "Most Beautiful Campus in the East," with three campuses including Suiyuan, Zijin and Xianlin.

始建于 1954 年,拥有仙林和汉中门两个校区,被誉为"中国高等中医教育的摇篮"。

Founded in 1954, with campuses of Xianlin and Hanzhongmen, known as "the Cradle of Chinese TCM Higher Education."

国家"211 工程"、国家"985 工程"大学,拥有鼓楼、浦口、仙林三个校区,被誉为"中国最温和的大学"。

It was chosen by the Central Government of China under the Project 211 and Project 985, known as the "Most Gentle University in China."

国家"985 工程"和"211 工程"重点建设的大学之一,有四牌楼、九龙湖等主校区,有着"学府圣地"和"东南学府第一流"的美誉。

It was chosen by the Central Government of China under Project 211 and Project 985, with campuses such as Sipailou, Jiulonghu, etc. and known as an "Institution of Learning" and "Top University in the Southeast."

3. 单人活动　Individual Work

你的国家有哪些著名学府?

What universities in your own country are famous for?

☞ 文化贴士6

第二章 扬州市
Chapter Two Yangzhou City

扬州,简称扬,是江苏省中部地区的中心城市,总面积 6 634 平方公里,全市总人口 461.34 万(2014 年)。扬州市南临长江,北接淮水,中贯大运河,有"淮左名都"之称,又有着"大运河第一城"的美誉。

Yangzhou, short for Yang, is a city in the Central District of Jiangsu Province and covers a total area of 6,634 square kilometers with a population of 4.61 million (2014). It borders the bank of the Yangtze River on the south, Huaihe River on the north and with the Grand Canal running across in the middle. It is known as "the Famous City East of the Huaihe River" and "the First City Along the Grand Canal."

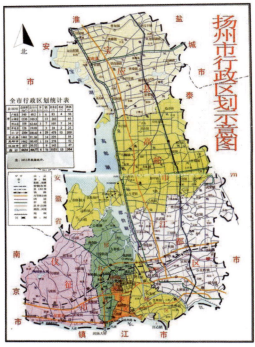

图 2 - 1 扬州市行政区划示意图

Chart 2 - 1 Administrative Division Map of Yangzhou

Part Two   Cities in Jiangsu Province

扬州是中国首批 24 座历史文化名城之一,有着 2 500 年建城史。历史上经历了西汉、晚唐和清初三次鼎盛时期。公元前 486 年,吴王夫差开**邗沟**①,筑邗城,开启了扬州的建城史。西汉为扬州历史上的第一次发展高峰。隋炀帝开凿大运河,确立了扬州的交通枢纽地位。盛唐时期的扬州雄富冠天下,时有"扬一益二"之称。清代中期,扬州成为漕运枢纽和全国最大的盐业经销中心,成为全世界 10 个拥有 50 万以上居民的大城市之一。

Yangzhou is one of the first 24 cities that were announced as historical and cultural cities in China with the history of 2,500 years. In its long history, Yangzhou has experienced splendid prosperity in the Western Han Dynasty, the late Tang Dynasty and the early Qing Dynasty. In 486 B.C., Fuchai, King of Wu State, excavated the Hangou Canal and built the Han City, which started the history of Yangzhou city. Yangzhou experienced splendid prosperity in the West Han Dynasty. It was renowned as the richest in the world during the Tang Dynasty and people had the saying "Yangzhou first, Yizhou second." During the middle period of the Qing Dynasty, Yangzhou became the water transportation center and the largest salt distribution center. The city topped as one of the ten largest cities in the world with a population of over half million.

① 邗沟是联系长江和淮河的古运河,是最早有明确记载的运河。

The Hangou Canal is an ancient canal linking the Yangtze River and the Huaihe River. It is the earliest recorded canal.

图 2 - 2　扬州古运河地图
Chart 2 - 2　Map of Yangzhou Ancient Canal

扬州是人文荟萃的文化名城,其经济的几度繁荣催生了灿烂的文化。许多著名诗人和学者如李白、杜牧、白居易、欧阳修、苏轼、郑板桥和朱自清等都在扬州留下足迹。鉴真大师东渡、崔致远入扬求学、普哈丁来扬传教、马可·波罗来扬任职,见证了扬州在中外交流史上的重要地位;漆器、玉器、剪纸、盆景等表现了扬州地方手工艺的高超水平;扬剧、清曲、弹词、评话等是扬州曲艺文化的独特代表;三把刀、淮扬菜、澡堂展示了扬州饮食沐浴休闲文化的精致;瘦西湖、个园、何园等见证了扬州盐商园林文化的繁荣。

本章主要从扬州历史与文化的角度去展示扬州这个运河名城和国际美食之都。

Yangzhou is a famous cultural city where many talented persons gather. A prosperous economy gave birth to splendid culture. A large number of well-known poets and scholars, such as Libai, Du Mu, Bai Juyi, Ouyang Xiu, Su Shi, Zhen Banqiao, Zhu Ziqing, etc. left their footprints on the city. Monk Jian Zhen's journey to Japan, Cui Zhiyuan's coming to study, Pu Hading's coming to preach and Marco Polo's appointed as an official in Yangzhou are testimonials to the important position of Yangzhou in the history of Chinese international communication. Lacquer ware, jade, paper-cutting, bonsai, etc. represent the high level of Yangzhou's local handicrafts. Yangzhou Opera, Yangzhou Ditty, *Tanci* and Yangzhou storytelling are the unique representatives of Yangzhou's Quyi culture. Three knives, Huaiyang Cuisine and bathhouses present the elegance of Yangzhou's leisure culture. While Slender West Lake, Geyuan Garden and Heyuan Garden witnessed the prosperity of Yangzhou salt merchants' garden culture.

This chapter presents Yangzhou from historical and cultural aspects, to display the famous Canal City and City of Gastronomy.

第一节　运河文化

Unit One　Grand Canal Culture

中国大运河是世界上最长的人工运河。2014 年 6 月 22 日,在第 38 届世界遗产大会上获准列入世界遗产名录,成为中国第 46 个世界遗产项目。中国大运河由京杭大运河、隋唐大运河和浙东大运河三部分组成,全长 2 700 公里。

The Grand Canal of China is the longest canal in the world. On June 22，2014，the Grand Canal was officially approved to be a site written into the list of world cultural heritage sites and became China's 46th world heritage site. The sections included in the site of the Grand Canal are comprised of three parts—Beijing-Hangzhou Grand Canal，Sui-Tang Dynasties' Grand Canal and East Zhejiang Grand Canal，with a total length of 2,700 kilometers.

图 2 - 3　京杭大运河示意图

Chart 2 - 3　Map of Beijing-Hangzhou Grand Canal

京杭大运河,通常简称为大运河,是世界上开凿时间最早、里程最长的人工运河。大运河北起涿郡(今北京),南到余杭(今杭州),途经北京、天津两市及河北、山东、江苏、浙江四省,贯通海河、黄河、淮河、长江、钱塘江五大水系,全长1 797 公里,是苏伊士运河(190 千米)的 9 倍,巴拿马运河(81.3 千米)的 22 倍。运河对中国南北地区之间的经济、文化发展与交流,特别是对沿线地区工农业经济的发展起了巨大作用。与长城、坎儿井并称为中国古代的三项伟大工程,并且使用至今。

Beijing-Hangzhou Grand Canal, generally called the Grand Canal for short, is the longest and oldest ancient artificial canal in the world. Starting from Zhuojun(Beijing) in the north to Yuhang (Hangzhou) in the south. It crosses Beijing, Tianjin, Hebei Province, Shandong Province, Jiangsu Province and Zhejiang Province, and connects the Haihe River, Yellow River, Huaihe River, Yangtze River and Qiantang River. The total length of Beijing-Hangzhou Grand Canal is 1,797 kilometers, which is 9 times longer than Suez Canal (190 kilometers), and 22 times longer than Panama Canal (81.3 kilometers). The Grand Canal is a great contribution to the south north economic trade as well as the cultural and political integration. Especially it largely promotes the industrial and agricultural development on both sides. Together with the Great Wall and Kariz (a popularized and traditional water conservancy and irrigation system in northwest China mainly in Xinjiang Autonomous Region), it is known as one of the three greatest ancient projects of China and is currently still in service.

 运河历史 History of the Grand Canal

大运河始凿于春秋①末期。公元前 486 年,吴王夫差进军北上伐齐,为屯军储粮,开邗沟,沟通江淮间水道,这一段是最早见于明确记载的运河;于蜀冈上筑邗城,为扬州建城之始。公元 605 年,隋炀帝利用天然河道和旧有渠道,到公元 610 年开通了北起涿郡、南至余杭的大运河。经元朝修会通河和通惠河以后就成为以大都为中心的长达1 797 千米的京杭大运河了。在漫长的历史时期里,大运河都是中国南北交流和交通的主要通道,并促进了文化交流与政治融合。19 世纪中叶以后,因为战争和自然因素,一些河段淤塞断流,大运河地位衰退。然而,江苏和浙江境内河段仍继续保持通航。铁路航空运输方式

① 春秋时期是中国历史阶段之一,一般指的是公元前 770 年—公元前 476 年,此时也是希腊、古罗马文化的鼎盛时期。

The Spring and Autumn Period was a period in Chinese history from approximately 771 to 476 B. C. It was also the period when the culture of ancient Geek and Rome flourished.

的发展使大运河运输重要性逐渐减弱,但大运河丰富的历史文化遗存是中华悠久历史文明的最好见证。如今,中国南水北调工程为大运河发展带来了新机遇,其东线工程即利用京杭大运河作为长江水北送的主要渠道。

The Grand Canal was launched in the late Spring and Autumn Period. In 486 B. C., King Fuchai, ruler of the State of Wu (present-day Suzhou), ventured north to conquer the neighboring State of Qi. In order to transport his troops and grain by water, he opened the historically famous Hangou to connect the waterways among Yangtze River and Huaihe River, by means of the natural waterway systems. This was the earliest record of the Grand Canal in history. Fuchai also built Hancheng Castle on Shugang in today's Yangzhou. In 605 A. D. Emperor Yangdi of the Sui Dynasty began to extend and expand the existing canals and waterways, and by 610 A. D. the Grand Canal was finished that started at Zhuojun in the north and terminated at Yuhang in the south. During the Yuan Dynasty (1271—1368) the entire 1,797-kilometer length of the Grand Canal, as we know today, was completed where the Huitong River and Tonghui River flowed to the Yuan capital, Dadu (Beijing). During the long period of history, as the main waterway for communications and transportation, the Grand Canal enabled cultural exchange and political integration between the north and south of China. After the mid-19th century, it declined because of warfare and natural factors—some sections silted up or fell into decay. However, the section inside Jiangsu and Zhejiang continues in service. Although the development of rail and air transport weakened the importance of water transportation, the rich historic and cultural relics of the Grand Canal best witnessed the advanced civilization in China's history. At present, South-to-North Water Diversion Project brings new opportunities to it. The East Route Project is the main channel which diverts water from Yangtze River to the north by virtue of the Grand Canal.

运河水不仅承载着南来北往的船只,而且孕育了一批文化名城。而扬州是唯一与大运河同生共长、兴衰与共的城市。扬州城池的变迁,城市水系的变化,都与历代大运河有着密切联系。扬州位于长江与运河的交汇处,因其地理优势,扬州一直是封建王朝的漕运和盐运中心,在唐代达到鼎盛,成为当时中国除长安(今西安)、洛阳之外最繁荣的国际大都会和贸易中心。清代扬州呈现出由大运河盐运为主体的盐业经济特征,瘦西湖、扬州盐业历史遗迹、天宁寺等均是这种经济格局留下的实物见证。

The Grand Canal was not only a waterway for transportation, but also gave birth to many famous cultural cities along the canal. Yangzhou is the only city which grows, prospers and declines with the canal. The development of the city and the change of the city water system are connected with the canal closely. Yangzhou is located where the Grand Canal meets the Yangtze River. Because of the geographical advantages, it remained as an important center for river transportation and salt transport throughout the imperial dynasties. The city reached its peak during the Tang Dynasty, when it was China's most prosperous metropolis and trade center besides Chang'an (Xi'an) and Luoyang. In the Qing Dynasty, salt transport by means of the Grand Canal became the main body of the economic development in Yangzhou. Slender West Lake, remains of the Salt industry, and the Tianning Temple are the witnesses of this economic pattern.

图 2 - 4　扬州运河地图

Chart 2 - 4　Map of the Grand Canal in Yangzhou

千百年来,大运河的开凿使扬州成为一个帝王、富商和名人的流连之地。隋炀帝(569—618)曾三下扬州;清朝的康熙皇帝(1654—1722)、乾隆皇帝(1711—1799)六下江南,每次都从运河乘龙舟到扬州。清代盐商为了取悦皇帝,广建名园,为扬州留下了丰富的园林文化遗产。普哈丁园是外来宗教随大运河来到扬州,并与本土文化结合形成扬州多元文化的物证。东关街是扬州城和大运河发展演变的历史见证,是扬州大运河文化与盐商文化的发祥地和展示窗口,佐证着扬州城曾经的经济繁荣和文化昌盛。

For a thousand years after the opening of the Grand Canal, Yangzhou was a pleasure and recreation destination for emperors, the wealthy and the famous. Emperor Yangdi(569—618)of the Sui Dynasty visited Yangzhou three times, and the Qing emperors Kangxi(1654—1722)and Qianlong(1711—1799)each made six inspection tours to South China, with Yangzhou as a major stop. Salt merchants in the Qing Dynasty competed to please the emperors by building garden villas for them, leaving the city with a rich legacy of different gardens. The Tomb of Pu Hading was the witness which foreign religion spread and blended with local culture to form cultural diversity in Yangzhou. As a history testimony of the development of Yangzhou City and the Grand

图 2 - 5　扬州列为"立即列入项目"10 项遗产点示意图

Chart 2 - 5　Sketch Map of 10 Heritage Sites "Immediately Listed Projects" in Yangzhou

Canal, a birthplace and showcase of Grand Canal culture and salt merchants culture，Dongguan Street gave an evidence of economic boom and cultural prosperity of Yangzhou in the past.

作为大运河的发源地，大运河申遗成功后，扬州共有 6 段河道、10 个遗产点列入首批申遗点段，成为沿线运河城市中入选世界遗产名录最多的城市。

As the cradle of the Grand Canal，there are 6 river sections and 10 heritage sites in Yangzhou which are listed as world heritage. Yangzhou has the most world heritage selected among the cities along the canal.

二 湖上园林——瘦西湖
Classical Lake Garden—Slender West Lake

Slender West Lake

瘦西湖位于扬州市西北郊，是扬州最大的湖上园林，也是大运河上独特的文化景观。

The Slender West Lake lies in the northwest suburb of Yangzhou City. It is the largest water garden in Yangzhou and a unique cultural landscape along the Grand Canal.

瘦西湖原是一条称为"保障河"的自然湖泊，自隋唐时期陆续沿湖建园，到清**乾隆**②年间（1736—1795）达到鼎盛。

The Slender West Lake used to be a natural river named Baozhang. Gardens were constructed in succession since the Sui and Tang Dynasties and reached the peak in the reign of Emperor Qianlong of the Qing Dynasty （1736—1795）.

② 乾隆（1711—1799），是清朝第六代皇帝，是中国历史上实际执掌国家最高权力时间最长的皇帝。
Emperor Qianlong, the sixth emperor of the Qing Dynasty who had the longest reign in Chinese history.

Great Rainbow

瘦西湖最主要、最具特色的五个景区是长堤春柳景区、小金山景区、五亭桥和白塔景区、二十四桥景区、万花园景区。

The five most important and characteristic scenic spots are the Long Embankment Among Spring Willows，the Little Golden Hill，

Five Pavilions Bridge and White Pagoda，Twenty-Four Bridges，All-Flower Garden.

Xuyuan Garden

Little Golden Hill

瘦西湖园林建造风格既有北方之雄伟，又有南方之秀丽。

The construction style of the Slender West Lake is its marvelous harmony of northern grandiosity and the southern elegance.

Twenty-Four Bridges

Xichun Terrace

 宗教遗产——大明寺
Religious Heritage—Daming Temple

Daming Temple

大明寺位于扬州市西北郊的蜀冈风景区，是这座城市最古老的寺庙之一，有着1 500多年历史。

Daming Temple is located in the Shugang Scenic Area in the northwest suburb of Yangzhou. It is one of the most ancient temples in the city，with a history of more than 1,500 years.

大明寺始建于南朝宋孝武帝大明年间，故称大明寺。

Daming Temple was first built during the reign of Daming

Archway

Pingshan Hall

③ 鉴真（688—763），唐代僧人，生于扬州，是中国律宗祖师，日本佛教律宗开山祖师。

Jian Zhen（688—763），a monk in the Tang Dynasty, was born in Yangzhou. He was a Chinese Vinaya master and the founder of Japanese Vinaya.

④ 平山堂得名于坐此堂上，江南诸山，历历在目，似与堂平。

Pingshan Hall is thus named because it appears to be higher in elevation than all other hill tops. It offers an unblocked view of all the hills of the South.

No. 5 Spring Under Heaven

（457—464），the Southern Song Emperor Xiao Wu, hence named Daming.

牌楼位于大明寺前的广场，在古树掩映之中，上面刻有"栖灵遗址"四个字。

In front of Daming Temple, there is an ancient decorated archway amidst the ancient trees, bearing the inscription of "Ruins of Xiling."

寺内佛教殿堂有：天王殿、大雄宝殿、卧佛殿、藏经楼、钟鼓楼、栖灵塔、**鉴真**③纪念堂；文化古迹有：欧阳修所筑的**平山堂**④以及他的学生苏轼为纪念他而建的谷林堂等。大明寺西侧是著名的西园、园内有天下第五泉等景点。

The main Buddhist constructions in Daming are laid out along the central axis. They are the Heavenly King Hall, Mahavira Hall, Hall of Reclining Buddha, the Scripture House, the Bell and Drum Tower, Xiling Tower and the Memorial Hall of the Master Jian Zhen. There are also many cultural relics, such as Pingshan Hall built by Ouyang Xiu and Gulin Hall built by Su Shi to commemorate his teacher Ouyang Xiu. A royal garden of the Qing Dynasty with "No. 5 Spring Under Heaven" is located in the west of Daming Temple.

Jian Zhen Memorial Hall

Xiyuan Garden

 四　盐业遗迹——个园
Remains of Salt Industry—Geyuan Garden

个园位于扬州的东关街上,由清代盐商黄至筠建于 1818 年,是保存得最好的一处私家园林。

Geyuan Garden, on Dongguan Street in Yangzhou, was built by the salt tycoon, Huang Zhiyun, in 1818 in the Qing Dynasty. Today it is a well-preserved private garden.

个园以四季假山著称,是中国明清私家园林的经典代表。春山由竹林里的石笋组成,代表雨后春笋。

Geyuan Garden is well-known especially for its "Four Season Hills." It is a classic representation of private gardens from the Ming and Qing Dynasties. Spring Hill is composed of rock pinnacles amidst bamboo groves, which stand for bamboo shoots after a spring rain.

夏山是一组玲珑剔透的湖石假山,中间以曲径和石洞相通。

Summer Hill is a cluster of small, shallow ponds and rockeries connected by hidden caves and passageways.

秋山由红褐色、棱角分明的黄山石堆叠,以形成悬崖峭壁。

Autumn Hill is made of red-brown, irregular-shaped rocks from Mount Huangshan, arranged to mimic sheer cliffs.

冬山由宣石堆叠而成,晶莹雪白,闪闪发光。

Winter Hill is made up of pure-white rocks that glisten in the

思考 Question

为什么称为个园?
Why did the garden get its name "Geyuan Garden"?

sunlight and look as white as snow.

Spring Hill

Summer Hill

Autumn Hill

Winter Hill

 烟火市井——东关街

Old Yangzhou Alley—Dongguan Street

 思考 **Question**

请问你知道扬州还有哪些历史街区吗?

Do you know what other historical areas of the ancient Yangzhou are?

东关街,位于扬州明清古城东北角,是扬州城里最具代表性的一条历史老街。它东至**古运河**边,西至国庆路,全长1 122米。

Dongguan Street is situated at the northeast corner in ancient part of the city of Yangzhou from the Ming and Qing Dynasties. Its most representative ancient alley is in the center of Yangzhou. It is east of the Grand Canal and west of Guoqing Road with a

Pot Garden

Wudang Palace

Dongrong Gareden

total length of 1,122 meters.

东关街东首是扬州城唐宋东门遗址和大运河扬州东关古渡。因此，东关街从前不仅是扬州水陆交通要道，而且是商业、手工业和宗教文化中心，至今仍延续着明清建筑风格。

In the eastern part of the city there is the east gate of Yangzhou city from the Tang and Song Dynasties and the Yangzhou Dongguan old ferry of the Grand Canal. In the past, Dongguan Street was not only a stop on water and land transportation routes in Yangzhou, but also the center of business, handicrafts and religious culture. Today, it still retains architectural styles from the Ming and Qing Dynasties.

东关街人文古迹众多，在这里既可以参观历史遗址、园林、盐商大宅、寺庙、古街巷，独特的运河风光和地方风情，也可以欣赏地方文化艺术、传统民间手工技艺，体验扬州休闲生活方式。

Changle Inn

The Yipu Garden

Dongguan Street is endowed with abundant historical and cultural resources. Here we can appreciate not only numerous

famous historical sites and gardens，magnificent mansions and temples，ancient streets and lanes，the Grand Canal and local customs of the city，but also enjoy the local culture and arts，traditional folk craftsmanship and leisure style of Yangzhou.

任务　Tasks

1. 小组活动　Group Work

扬州园林有2 000多年历史,在清代康乾年间达到鼎盛。查找相关资料了解扬州园林的特点并说说你所在城市的园林。

Yangzhou has been known for its private classical gardens for over 2,000 years, and they enjoyed their golden age during the Qing Dynasty under the emperors Kangxi and Qianlong. Please find out related information to understand the characteristics of Yangzhou gardens and talk about the gardens in the city where you live.

提示(Clues)：

扬州园林既具有皇家园林的雄伟壮丽,又有江南园林的精致秀美,自成一种风格。

Yangzhou gardens have their own style, that is, a combination of magnificence and grandiosity of royal gardens in the north with elegance and exquisiteness of private gardens in the south.

2. 单人活动　Individual Work

你知道这些景点的名字吗?

Do you know the names of the following scenic spots?

平山堂
Pingshan Hall

第五泉
No. 5 Spring Under Heaven

欧阳祠
Ouyang Shrine

鉴真坐像
Sitting Statue of Jian Zhen

牌楼
Archway

栖灵塔
Xiling Tower

3. 小组活动　Group Work

请和你的朋友一起游览东关街后填写下面表格。

Please fill in the following table after visiting Dongguan Street.

文化古迹 Cultural Attractions			
"老字号"商家 Time-Honored Shops			
东关美食 Dongguan Cuisine			
特色住宿 Lodging			

第二节　淮扬佳肴
Unit Two　Huaiyang Food

淮安、扬州是国家历史文化名城。淮扬菜系指以明清时期淮安府和扬州府为中心的淮扬地域性菜系。淮扬菜,始于春秋,兴于隋唐,盛于明清,素有"东南第一佳味,天下之至美"之美誉。

隋代完工的京杭大运河流经江苏省的淮安、扬州等地。大运河的贯通促进了水路运输的快速发展以及盐运经济的繁荣。盐商奢华的生活方式刺激了淮扬菜的发展。淮扬菜在清代达到顶峰,当时的康熙、乾隆皇帝每次下江南都要到淮安和扬州。地方官员为了取悦皇帝而准备美味佳肴,极大地推动了地方菜系发展。

Huai'an and Yangzhou are national historical and cultural cities. Huaiyang Cuisine refers to the local dish styles with Huai'an prefecture and Yangzhou prefecture as centers during the Ming and Qing Dynasties. Huaiyang Cuisine originated from the Spring and Autumn period, rose in the Tang and Song Dynasties and flourished in the Ming and Qing Dynasties. It has long been known as "the first delicacy in the southeast, the best taste in the world."

The Grand Canal which was built in the Sui Dynasty stretched from Beijing to Hangzhou and ran through Huai'an and Yangzhou in Jiangsu Province. Water transport developed rapidly along with the construction of the Grand Canal, which in turn caused a boom in the salt transportation business. The extravagant lifestyle of rich salt merchants greatly stimulated the development of Huaiyang Cuisine. Huaiyang Cuisine reached its peak in the Qing Dynasty when the Emperors Kangxi and Qianlong stayed in Huai'an and Yangzhou during their visits to southern China. It is said that local officials in charge of water transport used to prepare complex mutton and eel dishes to please the emperors, greatly boosting the development of the local cuisine.

一　淮扬菜系 Huaiyang Cuisine

Crab Powder Ball

Wensi Toufu

淮扬菜系，又称为江苏菜系，是中国四大菜系之一。

Huaiyang Cuisine, also called Jiangsu Cuisine, is considered to be amongst one of the Four Great Cuisines.

淮扬菜是长江中下游地区的著名菜系，始于江淮地区，主要分淮扬、金陵、苏锡、徐海风味。扬州、淮安是公认的淮扬菜的故乡。

Huaiyang Cuisine is derived from the native cooking styles of the region surrounding the lower reaches of the Huaihe River and the Yangtze River，and gets popular in the lower reach of the Yangtze River. It consists of the styles of Huaiyang, Jinling, Suxi and Xuhai dishes. Yangzhou and Huai'an are considered to be the birthplaces.

Squirrel-Shaped Mandarin

Boiled Salted Duck

淮扬菜刀功非常精细，尤以瓜雕享誉四方。淮扬菜原料多以水产为主，刀工细腻，口味清淡平和，咸甜浓淡适中，南北皆宜。

The carving techniques of Huaiyang Cuisine are very intricate, of which the melon carving technique is especially well-known. Raw materials of Huaiyang dishes include fresh and live aquatic

products. The flavor of Huaiyang Cuisine is light, fresh and sweet, an aromatic mix of northern and southern tastes.

淮扬菜曾多次走入国宴，始于 1949 年中华人民共和国开国大典首次盛宴。

Huaiyang Cuisine has been used for official occasions by Chinese government, even for the first state banquet of the People's Republic of China in 1949.

二 扬州美食 Yangzhou Famous Food

扬州文化内涵十分丰富，尤其是其饮食文化，历史上就有"吃在扬州"的美誉。

Yangzhou is famous for its rich cultural connotation, especially culinary culture, known as "eating in Yangzhou."

扬州美食属于中国四大菜系之一的淮扬菜系，兴起于隋朝，有 1 200 年历史。

Yangzhou food belongs to the Huaiyang Cuisine, one of the four best-known cuisines in China. It first appeared in the Sui Dynasty（581—618）and has a history of 1,200 years.

扬州名宴主要有三头宴、满汉全席、红楼宴等。

The famous banquets of Yangzhou include the Three-Head

Fuchun Teahouse

Banquet，the Manchurian and Chinese Delicacies，and the Banquet of the Red Mansion.

扬州著名菜品有大煮干丝、文思豆腐、蟹粉狮子头等。

Famous Yangzhou dishes mainly include Braised Shredded Chicken with Ham and Dried Tofu，Wensi Tofu Soup，and Crab Powder Meat Ball.

扬州名点有扬州炒饭、富春包子等。

Famous desserts of Yangzhou include Yangzhou Fried Rice，Fuchun Steamed Bun and so on.

扬州美食街有文昌美食广场、望月路美食街、四望亭美食街等。

The food street includes Wenchang Food Plaza，Wangyue Road Pedestrian Street and Siwang Pagoda Food Street.

扬州有很多餐饮名店，如富春茶社、西园大酒店、迎宾馆、扬州京华大酒店等。

There are many famous restaurants in Yangzhou：the Fuchun Teahouse, the Xiyuan Hotel，the Yangzhou State Guesthouse，and the Grand Metropole Hotel，etc.

任务　Tasks

1. 小组活动　Group Work

为下图不同地方风味的淮扬菜品找到正确的名称。

Find the right names for these Huaiyang dishes in the pictures.

盐水鸭 Salted Duck（mainly popular in Nanjing）	脆皮银鱼 Crispy Whitebait（mainly popular in Wuxi）
羊方藏鱼 Fish Wrapped in Mutton（mainly popular in Xuzhou）	松鼠鳜鱼 Braised Squirrel-Shaped Mandarin（mainly popular in Suzhou）
文思豆腐 Wensi Tofu（mainly popular in Yangzhou）	炒软兜 Fried Eel（mainly popular in Huai'an）

2. 小组活动　Group Work

看图，将列表中的信息与图片连起来。

Look at the pictures and match the information in each table.

相传隋炀帝下扬州命令名厨烹制这道菜品，主要由鲜肉、蟹粉和蟹肉做成。

It is said that Emperor Yangdi of the Sui Dynasty issued order for famous cooks to make this dish during his trip to Yangzhou. It is made of meat, crab power and crab meat.

这道菜刀工要求极其精细，由切成细如发丝的豆腐干、鸡丝、笋丝等加鸡汤烹制而成。

This dish demands perfect way of slicing. It is made of bean curd sliced as thin as hair, sliced chicken, bamboo shoots boiled with chicken soup.

因清乾隆时期扬州天宁寺里文思和尚制作得名，主要由豆腐和火腿丝等做成。

It was named after its designer, the monk Wensi, from Yangzhou Tianning Temple during Qianlong's reign. It is made of tofu and sliced ham.

曾被称为"碎金饭"，隋炀帝巡幸江都时，也将其传入扬州。

It was formerly recorded as "broken gold rice." It is said that this dish has been passed to Yangzhou when the Emperor Yangdi of the Sui Dynasty patrolled to Jiangdu.

3. 单人活动　Individual Work

介绍一下自己国家的美食。

Please talk about the cuisine in your own country.

第三章　苏州市
Chapter Three　Suzhou City

☞ 文化贴士7

　　苏州,古称吴,简称为苏,又称姑苏、平江、东方威尼斯等,位于江苏省东南部,长江三角洲中部,东临上海、南接嘉兴、西抱太湖、北依长江。苏州下辖5个区,代管4市,全市面积8 488.42平方公里。

　　苏州物华天宝,人杰地灵,苏州城始建于公元前514年,有2 500多年历史。苏州是中国首批24座国家历史文化名城之一,是吴文化的发祥地。因其从古至今繁荣发达、长盛不衰的文化和经济,被誉为"人间天堂"、"丝绸之都(丝绸之府)"、"园林之城";又因其小桥流水人家的水乡古城特色,而有"东方威尼斯"、"东方水都(东方水城)"之称。苏州已经成为"城中有园"、"园中有城",山、水、城、林、园、镇为一体,古典与现代完美结合、古韵今风、和谐发展的国际化大都市,是江苏重要的经济、对外贸易、工商业和物流中心,是重要的文化、艺术、教育和交通中心。在飞速发展的城市现代化和国际化进程中,苏州对历史文化名城的保护工作也得到了国内外专家的广泛认可,苏州古城正以开放包容的文化姿态,成为凝聚各方创造热情、吸引国际关注的大舞台。

　　本章主要从苏州的工业园区经济与苏州旅游文化两个角度去展示苏州这个历史文化名城的魅力与活力。

　　Suzhou，called Wu in ancient times，referred to as Su，has also been called the Gusu，Pingjiang，Oriental Venice，etc. It is located in the southeast of Jiangsu Province，at the center of the Yangtze River Delta，the east of Shanghai and the south of Jiaxing. In the west is Taihu Lake and in the north the Yangtze River. Suzhou has five districts，hosting four cities，which covers an area of 8,488.42 square kilometers.

　　Suzhou is full of nature's treasures and outstanding people. It was built in 514 B. C. with more than 2,500 years of history. It was one of the first batch of 24 national historical and cultural cities in China. It is the birthplace of China's Wu Culture. Because of its historically prosperous culture and economy, it is known as "a paradise on earth," "the silk mansion" and "garden city." As it is famous for its small bridges in the ancient city, it's named the "Oriental Venice," or the "Oriental Waters City (Oriental Shuicheng)." Suzhou is entitled "gardens in a city" and "a city among gardens," with mountain, river, city, forest, garden and town all combined in a whole. It is a perfect combination of classic and modern, the ancient rhyme in modern time's style, and the international metropolis with a harmonious development. It's also the economic center of Jiangsu Province. Foreign trade, industry and commerce, logistics, as well as the core of culture, art and traffic, are all integral parts of it as a key tourism city in China. With rapid development in the process of modernization and internationalization, the protection of the historical and cultural city of Suzhou has been widely emphasized by experts at home and abroad. The ancient city of Suzhou holds an open and positive cultural attitude to inclusivism and attracting international attention to its stage.

This chapter mainly shows the charm and vitality of this historical and cultural city from the aspect of the economy of the industrial park in Suzhou and the tourism culture of the city.

第一节　工业园区

Unit One　Industrial Park

　　苏州是"苏南模式"的发源地。20 世纪 80 年代,苏州创造了以集体经济为主的乡镇企业发展模式,开启了苏南地区中国农村工业化的先河;90 年代,苏州把握了对外开放的机遇,大力发展外向型经济,促进了苏州经济质量的跃升;目前,苏州个体私营经济总量增长,民营经济撑起苏州经济半壁江山。

　　苏州是江苏省重要的经济、工商业、对外贸易和物流中心,也是全省重要的金融、文化、艺术、教育中心城市和交通枢纽城市,长江三角洲经济圈的中心城市之一。苏州的经济实力为全国地级市之首,居江苏省第一,紧逼北京、上海、广州、深圳。苏州的县域经济同样高度发达,下辖的张家港市、常熟市和昆山市在 2012 年官方公布的全国百强经济实力榜中,并列为全国百强县第一;下辖的太仓市则高居全国百强县第二。

　　苏州工业园区是中国和新加坡两国政府间合作的旗舰项目,改革开放试验田、国际合作示范区,中国发展速度最快、最具国际竞争力的开发区之一。苏州工业园区成为中国首个开展开放创新综合试验的地区。

　　2015 年,园区共实现地区生产总值 2 070 亿元,同比增长 8%;公共财政预算收入 257.2 亿元,增长 11.7%;税收占比达 93.6%,各类税收总收入超 670 亿元;进出口总额 796 亿美元,下降 0.9%;实际利用外资 16 亿美元;固定资产投资 612 亿元;R&D 投入占 GDP 比重达 3.35%;社会消费品零售总额 343 亿元,增长 10.5%;城镇居民人均可支配收入超 5.6 万元,增长 7.5%。园区发展质效持续优化提升。

　　园区约占苏州市 3.5% 的土地,5% 的人口,7% 的工业用电量以及 1% 的二氧化硫排放量和 2% 的 COD 排放量,创造了全市 15% 左右的 GDP、地方一般预算收入和固定资产投资,25% 左右的注册外资和进出口总额。园区已经成为苏州市经济社会发展的重要增长极,并得到了中新两国领导人的高度评价。

　　Suzhou is the birthplace of the "Southern Jiangsu Development Model." In the 1980s, Suzhou created a collective economy based on the development model of township enterprises, and set a precedent for China's rural industrialization in the South of Jiangsu. In the 1990s, Suzhou grasped at the opportunity to open to the outside world. It vigorously developed an export-oriented economy, and promoted the economic quality of Suzhou. Suzhou's private economy has experienced an incredibly fast growth, which has propped up half of the country's economy.

Suzhou is an important economic, industrial, foreign trade and logistic center of Jiangsu Province. It is also an important provincial financial, cultural, artistic and educational center, and a transportation hub city as well as one of the central cities of the Yangtze River delta economic circle. Suzhou's economy is at the forefront among prefecture-level cities of China, ranking the first in Jiangsu Province and only trailing nationally after Beijing, Shanghai, Guangzhou and Shenzhen. The local economy in Suzhou is also highly developed. Its jurisdictions of Zhangjiagang, Changshu and Kunshan were tied for the first place in the list of top 100 counties, which were officially announced in 2012. And the jurisdiction Taicang ranked second in the top 100 counties.

Suzhou Industrial Park is a flagship project mutually operated by China and Singapore. It's an open test field demonstrating the cooperation among nations and one of the fastest developed and the most competitive development zones in China. It has become the first innovative and comprehensive production area in China.

In 2015, Suzhou Industrial Park achieved a total regional GDP of 207 billion *yuan*, with a continuous year-on-year growth of 8%. The public finance budget revenue was 25.72 billion *yuan*, up 11.7% from the previous year. The total amount of taxes was over 67 billion *yuan*, accounting for 93.6% of local tax revenues. The total volume of imports and exports was US $79.6 billion, decreasing slightly by 0.9%. The incoming overseas capital reached US $1.6 billion. The fixed asset investment was 61.2 billion *yuan*. R&D investment accounted for more than 3.35% of the GDP. The total retail sale of social consumer goods was 34.3 billion *yuan*, increasing by 10.5%. Urban residents' disposable income was over 56,000 *yuan*, up by 7.5%. The development of quality and efficiency has continued to improve.

Suzhou Industrial Park accounts for about 3.5% of the land，5% of the population，7% of industrial electricity，1% of sulfur dioxide emissions and 2% of COD emissions in Suzhou，creating about 15% of the city's GDP and local general budget revenue and fixed asset investment，about 25% of the registered capital and total export-import volume. It has become an important part of the economic growth and social development of Suzhou City. It has got a great evaluation from Chinese and Singaporean leaders.

一 地理交通概况 Geographic Traffic

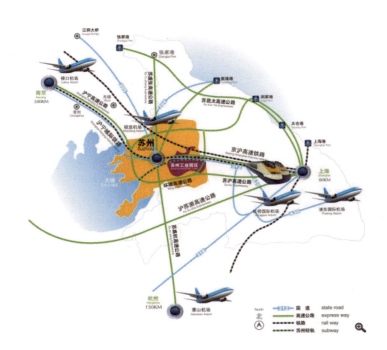

① 1994 年 5 月 12 日苏州工业园区首期开发建设正式启动。苏州工业园区总规划面积 288 平方公里，其中中新合作区 80 平方公里。

On May 12, 1994, the first phase of the construction and development of SIP officially started. The overall plan-ning area of Suzhou Industrial Park is 288 square kilometers, and the cooperation area of China and Singapore is 80 square kilometers.

② 沪、宁和杭分别是上海、南京和杭州的简称。

Hu, Ning and Hang refer to Shang-hai, Nanjing and Hangzhou respectively.

苏州工业园区①位于苏州古城区东部，以发达的高速公路、铁路、水路及航空网与世界各主要城市相连。

Suzhou Industrial Park is located in the eastern part of Suzhou ancient city，which is connected with the main cities of the world by the developed highway，railway，waterway and air networks.

轨道交通 20 分钟到达上海，60 分钟到达南京，与沪、宁、杭②融入同城轨道化生活。

People can get to and from Shanghai in about 20 minutes and Nanjing in about 60 minutes by rail transit from Suzhou. It is integrated into a great mega-city with Shanghai, Nanjing and Hangzhou.

在苏州市新制定的城市总体设计中,明确了苏州工业园区在"双城双片区"格局中的"苏州新城"地位,即把园区建设成为长三角地区重要的总部经济和商务文化活动中心之一。

According to the overall design of the new development regarding Suzhou, the status of Suzhou as "New City" should retain the pattern of "Twice the City in One Area." That is to build a park which acts as an important economic and cultural center of business activities in the Yangtze River Delta region.

发展成就 Development Achievements

苏州工业园区是中国发展速度最快、最具国际竞争力的开发区之一。主要经济指标年均增幅30%,综合发展指数位居国家级开发区第二位。园区转型升级成效显著,2013 年新兴产业产值 2 213 亿元,占规模以上工业比重 56.3%。

Suzhou Industrial Park is one of China's fastest growing and the most competitive development zones. With 30% annual average growth in key economic indicators, it ranks the second among national development zones in a comprehensive development index. In 2013, the output value of emerging industries was 221, 3 billion *yuan*, accounting for more than 56.3% of the industry scales because of the successful transformation and upgrading.

园区经过二十多年的建设与发展,利用外资连续多年名列中国开发区第一,先后被评为中国首批新型工业化示范基地、中国首批生态工业示范园区、中国首批国家知识产权示范创建园区、中国首个服务外包示范基地、中国首个鼓励技术先进型服务企业优惠政策试点区域、中国唯一服务贸易创新示范基地、中国唯一国家商务旅游示范区、中国唯一纳米技术创新及产业化基地,以及中国城市最具竞争力开发区排名第一等荣誉称号。

With more than 20 years of construction and development, Suzhou Industrial Park has ranked the first in the utilization of foreign capital for many years among Chinese development zones. It has been awarded as the first new-type industrial demonstration base in China. It is the first demonstration eco-industrial park, the first national intellectual property demonstration park, the first

service outsourcing demonstration base，the first experimental area on preferential policies for technologically advanced service enterprises，the only service trade innovation demonstration base，the only national business tourism demonstration area，as well as the only nanotech innovation and industrialization base and No. 1 of the most competitive development zones in China.

 入驻园区世界五百强企业
Top 500 Enterprises List in the Park

苏州良好的经济和社会发展态势，吸引了众多世界 500 强企业在苏州投资。截至 2014 年底，共有 147 家世界 500 强企业在苏州有投资项目（企业）。

With the healthy economic development，Suzhou has a good momentum that has attracted many of the world's top 500 enterprises to invest in Suzhou. By the end of 2014，altogether 147 world's top 500 enterprises had invested projects（corporations）in Suzhou.

序号 No.	国家 或地区 Country/ Area	企业 数量 No. of Corporation	企业名称 Corporation
1	美国 America	34	杜邦、埃克森美孚、辉瑞、礼莱、惠氏、卡夫、雪佛龙、施乐、陶氏化学、耐克、艾默生、霍尼韦尔、宝洁、阿彻丹尼尔斯米德兰、德尔福、明尼苏达矿业、美铝、泰科国际、强生、卡特彼勒、史泰博、国际纸业、联合技术、联合包裹、百事、摩根士丹利、乔治亚太平洋、通用汽车、戴姆勒、沃尔玛、通用电气、可口可乐、摩托罗拉、江森自控 DuPont, ExxonMobil, Pfizer, Eli Lily, Wyeth, Kraft Foods, Chevron, Xerox, Dow Chemical, Nike, Emerson, Honeywell, Procter&Gamble, Archer Daniels Midland, Delphi, Minnesota Mining and Manufacturing, Alcoa, Tyco International, Johnson & Johnson, Caterpillar, Staples, International Paper, United Technologies, United Parcel Service, PepsiCo, Morgan Stanley, Georgia Pacific, General Motors, Daimler AG, Wal-Mart, General Electric, Coca-cola, Motorola, Johnson Controls

续表

序号 No.	国家 或地区 Country/ Area	企业 数量 No. of Corporation	企业名称 Corporation
2	日本 Japan	42	三菱商事、三菱重工、三菱电机、三菱化学、三菱汽车、三井物产、三洋电机、丸红、伊藤忠、富士胶片、松下电器、丰田汽车、丰田自动织机、住友电工、住友商事、住友生命、索尼、夏普、日立、富士通、精工爱普生、旭化成、佳能、通运、日本电气、积水建房、新日本石油、新日铁、旭硝子、东芝、电装、小松、雅马哈、神户制钢、新日矿、五十铃汽车、普利司通、永旺、爱信精机、大和房建、第一生命、日本邮船 Mitsubishi, Mitsubishi Heavy Industries, Mitsubishi Electric, Mitsubishi Chemical, Mitsubishi Motors, Mitsui, Sanyo Electric, Marubeni, Itochu, Fuji Film, Panasonic, Toyota Motor, Toyota Industries, Sumitomo Electric, Sumitomo, Sumitomo Life, Sony, Sharp, Hitachi, Fujitsu, Seiko Epson, Asahi Kasei, Canon, Ton-Ying, Nippon Electric, Sekisui House, Nippon Oil, Nippon Steel, Asahi Glass, Toshiba, Denso, Komatsu, Yamaha, Kobe Steel, Nippon Mining, Isuzu Motors, Bridgestone, Aeon, Aisin Seiki, Daiwa House Industry, Daiwa House Industry, Dai-ichi Mutual Life, Nippon Yusen
3	法国 France	14	阿尔卡特朗讯、液化空气、阿海珐、欧莱雅、道达尔、欧尚、家乐福、达能、施耐德、拉法基、圣戈班、苏伊士、阿尔斯通、索迪斯联合 Alcatel-Lucent, Air Liquide, Areva, L'Oreal, Total, Auchan, Carrefour, Danone, Schneider, Lafarge, Saint-Gobain, Suez, Alston, Sodexho Alliance
4	英国 England	6	英国石油、葛兰素史克、联合利华、翠丰、力拓集团、英力士集团 British Petroleum, GlaxoSmithKline, Unilever, Kingfisher, Rio Tinto Group, Ineos
5	韩国 Korea	12	三星电子、浦项制铁、鲜京、SK Networks、现代汽车、现代重工、乐金电子、乐金显示、GS 控股、GS 加德士、韩华集团、斗山 Samsung, Pohang Steelers, Sunkyong, SK Networks, Hyundai Motor, Hyundai Heavy Industries, LG Electronics, LG Display, GS Holdings, GS Caltex, Hanwha, Doosan

续表

序号 No.	国家 或地区 Country/ Area	企业 数量 No. of Corporation	企业名称 Corporation
6	德国 Germany	13	西门子、博世、采埃夫、大众、巴斯夫、麦德龙、拜耳、大陆、贺利氏、林德、德国铁路、蒂森克虏伯、费森尤斯 Siemens, Bosch, ZF Friedrichshafen, Volkswagen, BASF, Metro, Bayer, Continental, Heraeus, linde, Deutsche Bahn, Thyssen Krupp, Fresenius
7	意大利 Italy	1	菲亚特 Fiat
8	荷兰 Holland	5	飞利浦、壳牌、阿克苏诺贝尔、利安德巴塞尔、荷兰国际 Philips, Shell, Akzo Nobel, LyondellBasell Industries, ING
9	瑞士 Switzerland	2	诺华、雀巢 Novartis, Nestle
10	芬兰 Finland	2	诺基亚、斯道拉恩索 Nokia, Stora Enso
11	挪威 Norway	1	海德鲁 Hydro
12	加拿大 Canada	3	加拿大铝业、玛格纳、庞巴迪 Alcan, Magna, Bombardier
13	瑞典 Sweden	1	爱生雅 SCA
14	丹麦 Denmark	1	马士基 Maersk
15	印度 India	1	塔塔汽车 Tata Motors
16	新加坡 Singapore	2	伟创力、丰益国际 Flextronics, Wilmar International
17	中国香港 Hong Kong	1	怡和洋行 Jardine Matheson
18	中国台湾 Taiwan	6	广达电脑、鸿海精密、华硕、台塑、仁宝、纬创集团 Quantacomputer, Hon Hai Precision Industry, Asus, Formosa, Palmax, Wistron
合计　Total		147	

任务　Tasks

单人活动　Individual Work

请点击"苏州工业园区"官网 http：//www.sipac.gov.cn/，按照发展规划图，连线指出以下数字所代表的区域。

Please click http：//www.sipac.gov.cn/ to find out the relevant district from the following map.

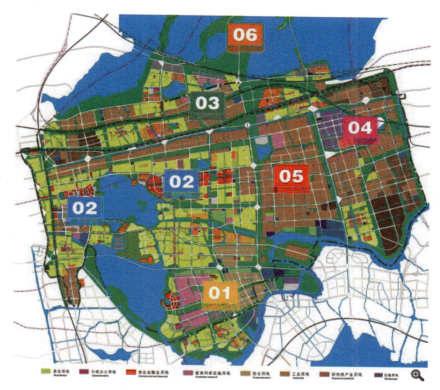

1. 阳澄湖生态旅游度假区 Yangcheng Lake Ecological Tourism Resort
2. 三期高新产业区 High Tech Industrial Zone Ⅲ
3. 综合保税区 Comprehensive Bonded Zone
4. 中新生态科技城 New Ecological Science and Technology City
5. 金鸡湖中央商务区 Jinji Lake Central Business District
6. 独墅湖科教创新区 Dushu Lake Science and Education Innovation Zone

第二节　园林之旅

Unit Two　Classical Gardens

　　苏州素有"园林之城"美誉。苏州园林源远流长,全盛时200多处园林遍布古城内外,至今保存完好的尚存数十处,代表了中国江南园林风格。其中沧浪亭、狮子林、拙政园和留园分别代表着宋(948—1264)、元(1271—1368)、明(1369—1644)、清(1644—1911)四个朝代的艺术风格,被称为苏州"四大名园"。苏州古典园林以其古、秀、精、雅、多而享有"江南园林甲天下,苏州园林甲江南"之誉,是苏州独有的旅游资源。

　　苏州古典园林历史绵延2 000余年,在世界造园史上有其独特的历史地位和价值。她以写意山水的高超艺术手法,蕴含浓厚的汉族传统思想和文化内涵,展示东方文明的造园艺术典范。苏州古典园林宅园合一,可赏,可游,可居,可以体验让人舒畅的生活。这种建筑形态的形成,是在人口密集和缺乏自然风光的城市中,人类依恋自然,追求与自然和谐相处,美化和完善自身居住环境的一种创造。

　　Suzhou is known as the "garden city." Suzhou gardens have a long history. During its heyday, more than 200 gardens were beautifully situated throughout the city, inside and outside. Today, dozens of them are still well preserved in Chinese Jiangnan garden style. The Canglang Pavilion, Lion Grove, Humble Administrator's Garden and Lingering Garden, known as the "Four Famous Gardens" in Suzhou, respectively represent the art style of the Song Dynasty (A. D. 948—1264), the Yuan Dynasty (A. D. 1271—1368), the Ming Dynasty (A. D. 1369—1644) and the Qing Dynasty (A. D. 1644—1911). The classical gardens are a unique tourism resource in Suzhou and enjoy a reputation of "Jiangnan gardens are the best in China, and Suzhou gardens are the best in Jiangnan" because of their antiquity, beauty, excellence and elegance.

Suzhou classical gardens have a unique historical position and value in the world with a history of more than 2,000 years. It shows the oriental civilization model of the gardening art by superb artistry of impressionistic landscapes and a strong Han People's traditional thought and culture. People can enjoy, travel, live and have a comfortable life experience in Suzhou's classical home gardens. This kind of architectural form appears throughout the city. Though it has a dense population and deficient natural scenery where human beings can still enjoy nature, pursue a life in harmony with nature, beautify and improve the city's living environment.

拙政园 Humble Administrator's Garden

拙政园位于苏州古城东北街178号,占地面积52 000平方米。这是一座始建于公元十五世纪初的古典园林,具有浓郁的江南水乡特色。经过几百年的苍桑变迁,至今仍保持着平淡疏朗、旷远明瑟的明代风格,被誉为"中国私家园林之最"。

Humble Administrator's Garden is located on No. 178 Northeast Street in Suzhou, with an area of 52,000 square meters. It is a classical garden founded in the early 15th century with a strong flavor of Jiangnan water features. After hundreds of years of vicissitudes of history, it still has been keeping a wide and boundless style of the Ming Dynasty, which is called "the best Chinese private garden."

拙政园始建于明正德四年(1509),御史王献臣归隐苏州,

思考 Question

你知道中国有哪四大名园吗?

Do you know the four famous gardens in China?

在元代古寺旧址建拙政园，王献臣亲自参与造园，建造历时 20 年，1530 年方才竣工。后被其子赌博输掉之后，几经衰落易主，后太平天国忠王李秀成攻占苏州，在拙政园增建了很多建筑，将其作为忠王府办公的场所。

The Humble Administrator's Garden was built in the fourth year of Zhengde in the Ming Dynasty（1509）. It was built on the site of an old temple of the Yuan Dynasty. The officer Wang Xianchen came back to Suzhou after his retirement and took part in building it himself. The Humble Administrator's Garden was completed in 1530 after 20 years of construction. Later，it was gambled away by Wang Xianchen's son. Under new ownership，it faded from it's former glory until Li Xiucheng，the King of Taiping Heavenly Kingdom，took ownership. He built a lot of new constructions as the office of Zhong Palace when he attacked and occupied Suzhou.

拙政园是世界文化遗产，中国四大名园之一。每年，数以百万计的中外游人前来观光旅游，他们陶醉在古老、文明的传统文化之中。

The Humble Administrator's Garden is a world cultural heritage，one of China's four greatest gardens. Every year，millions of Chinese and foreign tourists come to visit and revel in the traditional culture of the ancient civilization.

 留园 Lingering Garden

留园位于苏州古城西北的阊门外，始建于明万历二十一年（1593 年）。

Lingering Garden is located in the northwest of the ancient city of Suzhou，outside the gate，built in the 21st year

of Ming Wanli's reign（1593）.

留园占地 30 余亩，集住宅、祠堂、家庵、园林于一身，该园综合了江南造园艺术，并以建筑结构见长，善于运用大小、曲直、明暗、高低、收放等文化，吸取四周景色，形成一组组层次丰富，错落相连，有节奏，有色彩，有对比的空间体系。

Lingering Garden covers an area of 30 *mu*（about 20,000 square meters），with houses, ancestral halls, huts and gardens in it. It displays the art of Jiangnan gardening. It is well-known for its building structure，making full use of the size, shade，height, angle and other culturally important aspects drawn from the surrounding landscape. It forms rich layers, random connection, rhythmed and colorful space systems.

 三　同里 Tongli

同里隶属江苏省吴江市，位于太湖沿岸，古运河之东，八湖环抱，小镇有 15 条河，被分成 7 个小岛。小河的排列成"川"字形，49 座古桥使这些小岛连接成一个整体。

Tongli, which belongs to Wujiang in Jiangsu Province, is

located along the bank of Taihu Lake and to the east of the ancient canal surrounded by eight lakes. The town is divided into 7 small islands by 15 rivers arranged like the Chinese character "川", and connected by 49 ancient bridges, making these islands connected as a whole.

优美秀丽的同里小镇以其沃野良田和丰富的自然资源而素有"小东方威尼斯"之称。

The pretty and leisure town of Tongli boasts fertile fields and rich resources, thus crowned as "Small Oriental Venice."

明清时期建筑多、水乡小桥多、名人志士多是同里古镇的特点。同里有 38 处明清时期住宅，47 座寺庙和祠堂，大约 100 多处当地大户人家和权贵的住宅以及名人雅士的故居.

Tongli is characterized by a large number of architectures originating from the Ming and Qing Dynasties, small bridges and outstanding celebrities. Tongli boasts 38 residences remaining from the Ming and Qing Dynasties, 47 temples and ancestral halls, and over 100 residences of local rich and powerful people as well as many former celebrities.

任务　Tasks

1. 小组活动　Group Work

苏州目前对外开放的园林有 19 处，请查阅相关资料，找出苏州还有哪些古典园林，并和同学分享最感兴趣的景点。

There are 19 parks open to the public in Suzhou. Please consult related materials to find out what other classical gardens in Suzhou，and share the one you are most interested in with your classmates.

2. 单人活动 Individual Work

请自己查阅苏州旅游信息网，了解一下千年古镇周庄，并将列表中的信息与图片连起来。

Please consult the Suzhou Tourism Information Network to learn about Zhouzhuang, the Millennium Eldest Town. Then，look at the pictures and match the information with the pictures.

四季周庄：以水文化为背景，以本地民俗为特色，以国际时尚为元素，集中展示周庄优秀传统文化和浓郁水乡民俗风情。
The four seasons in Zhouzhuang, with a background of water culture，are characterized by local folklore. It displays an international fashion， showing Zhouzhuang's excellent traditional culture and rich folk customs.

渔鹰表演：在周庄，渔鹰捕鱼是一种古老而神奇的捕鱼方式。
The Osprey Performance：Using ospreys to catch fish is an ancient and magical fishing method in Zhouzhuang.

听昆曲：被誉为"百戏之祖"，中国最古老的剧种，是六百年前元代戏曲家顾坚所创。
The Kunqu Opera, known as the origin of Chinese opera，is the oldest opera in China. It was created by Gu Jian from the Yuan Dynasty 600 years ago.

环镇水上游：由特色画舫"万三号"、"周庄号"承运，融体验、休闲、观光为一体，是水乡古镇游的极佳选择之一。
The trip around the town, carried by the gaily-painted leisure-boats， "Wansan" and "Zhouzhuang" give a combination of experiences. They are a relaxing and pleasant way of touring the ancient town.

第四章　其他城市
Chapter Four　Other Cities

☞ 文化贴士8

① 吴承恩（1500年—1582年），中国明代杰出的小说家，是中国古典四大名著之一《西游记》的作者。

Wu Cheng'en，(1500—1582)，was a Chinese novelist，also the author of Journey of the West，one of the Four Great Classical Novels of Chinese literature.

周恩来（1898—1976），中国共产党和中华人民共和国的主要领导人，中国人民解放军主要创建人和领导人。中华人民共和国成立任政府总理。

Zhou Enlai (1898—1976)，was the main leaders of China Communist Party and the People's Republic of China，the founder and leader of China People's Liberation Army. He was also the first Premier of the People's Republic of China.

江苏是著名的水乡，水域比例全国第一，镇江境内长江和京杭大运河汇就中国"江河立交桥"坐标。一方水土养一方人。仁者乐山，智者乐水。水的最大特点是活性和灵性。江苏人天性聪慧、脑子灵活，爱读书、会读书。从古至今，江苏大地上可谓英才辈出，群星灿烂，江苏各地最津津乐道的就是那里产生过多少名人名家。仅苏州一地，历史上就出了50位状元。泰州是京剧大师梅兰芳的故乡，宿迁是项王故里，淮安的历史名人有韩信、吴承恩、周恩来①等。今天，江苏仍然是全国教育最发达、人才最集中的省份。

江苏人勤劳敬业、心灵手巧，这是江苏成为制造业基地的重要原因。目前江苏的建筑大军已是举世闻名。南通建筑队的足迹遍布各地。南通还有"中国近代第一城"之美誉，同时拥有**七个中国第一**②。清末状元，被并称为中国近代四大实业家之一的张謇先生对此做出了巨大贡献。无锡是全国"智慧城市"的排头兵，物联网技术体现在生活的各个细节。

2016年经中国国务院批准同意的《长江三角洲城市群发展规划》中，明确长三角城市群规划范围包括江浙沪皖三省一市。江苏省有9个地级市入选，分别是南京、无锡、常州、苏州、南通、盐城、扬州、镇江、泰州。长江三角洲城市群将联手打造具有全球影响力的世界级城市群。

本章从两汉文化发源地——徐州和新丝绸之路东端起点城市——连云港两个代表城市，从一个侧面展示江苏城市在中华文化传承以及中国经济发展中的重要作用。

Jiangsu is a land of water，with the highest rate of water covering area in China. The Yangtze River and the Beijing-Hangzhou Grand Canal meet in Zhenjiang. Human beings are shaped by the land and water around them. Everyone has his own taste（A true man loves mountains and a wise man loves seas. ）.

The most special characteristics of water are its flexibility and spiritualism. People in Jiangsu are smart and wise, loving reading and studying. Since ancient times, there have appeared plenty of celebrities and famous scholars. Take Suzhou as example, there are over 50 Number One Scholars in its history. Taizhou is the hometown of Mei Lanfang, a very famous artist of Peking Opera. Suqian is the hometown of Xiangyu, prominent marshal and the King of Kings during the late Qin Dynasty. Huai'an brought up many famous historical figures, including Han Xin, Wu Cheng'en and Zhou Enlai. At present, Jiangsu is a province with most developed education and most talents.

Jiangsu people is hardworking and diligent, smart and skillful, therefore, it becomes the leading province of manufacturing. Construction industry in Jiangsu gets popular around the world. Construction work by Nantong working team operates a global scale. Nantong enjoys the reputation of the First City in Modern China, and wins seven China's First. Zhang Jian, Zhuangyuan (Number One Scholars) in the late Qing Dynasty, made great contribution. He is one of four famous industrialists in modern China. Wuxi ranks top as a Smart City in China, and its network technology has infiltrated into people's daily life.

In 2016, the Yangtze River Delta Metropolitan Group Development Plan, approved by the State Council of China, clearly makes a statement that it includes Jiangsu, Zhejiang, Anhui and Shanghai (three provinces and one municipality). Nine cities are included, namely Nanjing, Wuxi, Changzhou, Suzhou, Nantong, Yancheng, Yangzhou, Zhenjiang and Taizhou. The cities in the Yangtze River Delta Metropolitan Group will work together to build the world-level and global influential city group.

The chapter selects Xuzhou, the origin of the Han Culture, and Lianyungang, the eastern starting point of the new Silk Road, therefore, to display the crucial role of Jiangsu in inheriting traditional Chinese culture and promoting economic development.

② 七个中国第一：第一所师范学校南通师范学校（1902年）、第一座博物馆南通博物苑（1905年）、第一所纺织学校南通纺织专门学校（1912年）、第一所刺绣学校女红传习所（1914年）、第一所戏剧学校伶工学社（1919年）、第一所盲哑学校狼山盲哑学校（1916年）、第一所气象站军山气象台（1916年）。

Seven China's First: the first normal school, Nantong Normal College in 1902; the first private museum, Nantong Mu-seum in 1905; the first textile school, Nantong Textile School in 1912; the first embroidery school, Needlework Training School in 1914; the first drama school, Actors Study Group in 1919; the first blind and dumb school, Nantong Langshan Blind and Dumb School in 1916; the first weather station, Junshan Weather Station in 1916.

第一节　丝绸之路
Unit One　Silk Road

连云港古称瀛洲,秦设朐县,唐建海州,素有"淮口巨镇"、"东海名郡"之美誉。连云港是新亚欧大桥东桥头堡,《西游记》文化发源地,中国优秀旅游城市和江苏三大旅游资源富集区之一。

连云港位于我国万里海疆中部,南连长三角,北接渤海湾,西依大陆桥,隔海东北亚,是全国首批 14 个沿海开放城市之一。

Lianyungang, also called Yingzhou in ancient China, was set as Qu County in the Qing Dynasty, and as Haizhou in the Tang Dynasty. It has long been known as the "great town of Huai Kou," and a "famous county in Eastern China." Lianyungang is a continental bridge facing northeast across the sea, the eastern bridgehead of Eurasia. It is the cultural birthplace of *The Pilgrimage to the West*. It's an excellent city to visit in China and one of the three major regions rich in tourism resources in Jiangsu Province.

Lianyungang is located in the central part of China's vast coastal areas. With the south bordering the Yangtze River Delta, and the North on Bohai Bay, it is one of China's first 14 coastal open cities.

一 古丝绸之路 Ancient Silk Road

连云港被誉为新亚欧大陆桥东桥头堡和新丝绸之路东端起点，是中国中西部地区最便捷、最经济的出海口。

Lianyungang is honored as the eastern bridgehead of the Eurasian continental bridge and the eastern starting point of the new silk road. It's the most convenient and economic port of China's central and western regions.

丝绸之路，并不是一条单一的道路，而是指中国与世界其他地区之间贯穿古今的海上和陆上通商以及文化交流的区域。中国的丝绸、瓷器、陶器、茶叶等大量珍贵产品和科学文化，除通过横贯大陆的陆上交通线路大量输往中亚、西亚和非洲、欧洲之外，也通过海上源源不断地销往东亚、大洋洲、美洲和世界各地。

The Silk Road was not only a single road, but referred to the region where China had onshore and offshore trade as well as cultural exchange with the rest of the world. Chinese silk, porcelain, pottery, tea and other precious products as well as scientific innovations were not only transported to Central Asia, West Asia, Africa and Europe via these transcontinental lines but also continuously exported to East Asia, Oceania, and later even to the America and around the world by sea.

二 张骞出使西域 Zhang Qian's Mission to the Western Regions

丝绸之路的名字来自中国沿线的丝绸贸易，贸易开始于汉代（公元前 207 年—公元 220 年）。中国古代的张骞被誉为"中国走向世界第一人"。

The name of the Silk Road derives from the lucrative trade of Chinese silk carried out along its path. The trade

began in the Han Dynasty（207 B. C.—A. D. 220）. In ancient China，Zhang Qian was regarded as "the first person of China to venture out into the world."

丝绸之路正式开始于西汉时期张骞出使西域,他在公元前 138 年和公元前 119 年两次出访,在拓展西域的贸易之路上起到了重要的作用。

The Silk Road formally started after Zhang Qian's visit as an envoy to the Western Region during the Han Dynasty. He went there twice，in 138 B. C. and again in 119 B. C. He played a vital role in developing the Silk Road.

张骞两次出使西域,奠定了汉在西域管治的基础,并逐渐将西域纳入汉朝版图。

Zhang Qian's two missions to the western regions laid the foundation for western Han governance， and gradually brought the Han Dynasty into the western regions.

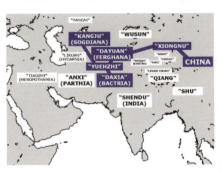

中西交通通道开辟后,西域的乐曲、乐器、舞蹈传入内地,希腊、罗马的雕刻和美术传入中国,扩大了汉人的艺术视野。另外,印度佛教和哲学也传入中国,除丰富了汉人的精神生活外,还对中国的宗教和艺术带来深远的影响。

After the opening of the Western trade channel from the East，China began cultural exchanges of music，instru-ments and dancing. These cultural exchanges extended as far east as Greece and the Roman Empire. Greek and Roman sculpture and art were

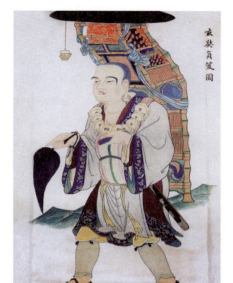

introduced into China，expanding the visual field of Chinese art. In addition，Indian Buddhism and philosophy were introduced into China，enriching the spiritual life of the Han people，as well as having profound influence on China's religion and art.

张骞的旅行促进了汉代和西部地区经济和文化交往。因为来自中国的丝绸成为占主导地位的交易产品，这个伟大的贸易路线后来称为丝绸之路。

Zhang Qian's journeys had promoted a great variety of economic and cultural exchanges between the Han Dynasty and the Western Regions. As silk gradually became the dominant product exported out of China，this great trade route later became known as the Silk Road or Silk Route.

唐代政府更加注重"丝绸之路"。不同于汉代丝绸之路，唐代控制了丝绸之路沿线的西部地区和中亚的一些地区，建立了有效且强大的政府部门，给中国的商人清除了障碍。

The Tang Dynasty government paid more attention to the Silk Road. Unlike the Silk Road in the Han Dynasty，the Tang Dynasty controlled over some areas of the Western Region and Central Asia along the road，establishing effective and sturdy orders，which cleared obstacles for Chinese businessmen.

中国著名的高僧玄奘在唐代开启沿丝绸之路的旅行。公元 366 年和 627 年他走

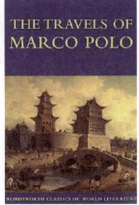

了克什米尔、巴基斯坦、印度和斯里兰卡等 30 多个国家，唐玄奘此行大大促进了唐朝政府与这些国家的友好关系。

The famous Chinese monk Xuan Zang twice traveled along the Silk Road during the Tang Dynasty from A.D. 366 to A.D. 627. Xuan Zang journeyed to more than 30 countries including Pakistan, India, Sri Lanka and so on. Xuan Zang's trip contributed greatly to the Tang government's friendly relations with the states in those regions at that time.

丝绸之路贸易在元朝时期达到了顶峰。著名旅行家马可·波罗沿着丝绸之路到达"大都"，就是今天的北京，写了著名的《马可·波罗游记》，向西方国家介绍了中国。

Trade along the Silk Road reached its zenith during the Yuan Dynasty. The famous traveler Marco Polo traveled along the Silk Road to visit Dadu, which is today's Beijing and wrote his famous book *The Travels of Marco Polo*, which popularized China in the western world.

三 一带一路 One Belt One Road

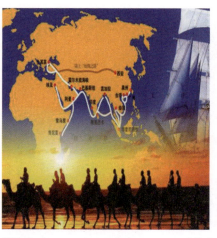

2013 年 9 月和 10 月，中国国家主席习近平在出访中亚和东南亚国家期间，先后提出共建"丝绸之路经济带"和"21 世纪海上丝绸之路"（以下简称"一带一路"）的重大倡议，得到国际社会高度关注。

When Chinese President Xi Jinping visited Central Asia and Southeast Asia in September and October of 2013, he suggested the re-establishment of a jointly-built Silk Road Economic Belt and the 21st-Century Maritime Silk Road (hereinafter referred to as the "One Belt One Road"), which has attracted attention from all over the world.

一带一路是连接亚洲、非洲和欧洲经贸往来的桥梁和纽带，关系到全球几十亿人口，这是人类历史上规模最大的综合发展规划项目之一。它将完善沿线国家的基础设施建设，譬如沿线公路、铁路、港口、

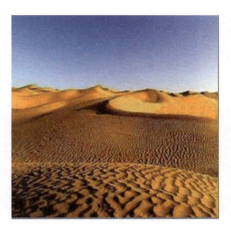

能源设施、健康医疗及教育等，为急需帮助的国家提供支援，实现共同发展，并将促进国家间投资、贸易和文化交流。

"One Belt One Road" would connect Asia, India and Europe in terms of trade that would affect billions of people around the globe. Together it would be one of the largest scale integrated development, which would ever be created. It would require highways, railroads, ports, energy facilities, health care and education. Collaborative growth would be achieved by providing assistance to countries in need. At the same time, it would also stimulate growth and international investment, commercial and cultural exchange.

新丝绸之路 New Silk Road

新丝绸之路是在古代"丝绸之路"的概念基础上形成的一个新的经济发展区域。它涵盖东南亚经济整合、东北亚经济整合，并最终融合在一起通向欧洲，形成欧亚大陆经济整合的大趋势。

Based on the concept of the ancient "silk road," the new silk road was formed as a kind of new economic development zone.

It would cover economic integration throughout southeast Asia, northeast Asia, and eventually fuse together with Europe, forming a complete Eurasian economic integration.

丝绸之路经济带，东边牵着亚太经济圈，西边系着欧洲经济圈，它被认为是"世界上最长、最有发展潜力的经济大走廊"。

The silk road economic belt would connect the Asia-Pacific economic circle in the east and the European econo-mic circle in the west. It is considered to be "the world's longest economic

corridor with the most potential for grand development."

"一带一路"战略将涵盖68个国家和地区的44亿人口,将产生21万亿美元的经济效应。

The "One Belt One Road" initiative would cover 68 countries and regions with a population of 4.4 billion people, and generate $21 trillion in economic gains.

除中国以外,"一带一路"还包括蒙古国、俄罗斯、中亚5国,东南亚11国,南亚8国,中东欧及南欧18国,独联体其他6国和西亚、北非16国。

Besides China, "One Belt One Road" would include Mongolia, Russia, 5 central Asian countries, 11 Southeast Asia countries, 8 South Asia countries, 18 central, eastern and southern Europe countries, as well as 6 countries in the Commonwealth of Independent States(CIS) and 16 countries in West Asia and North Africa.

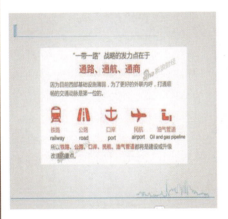

21世纪海上丝绸之路,从海上联通欧亚非三个大陆,最终可以和丝绸之路经济带形成一个海上、陆地的闭环。

The Maritime Silk Road in the 21st century would form a union between Mainland China, Europe and North Africa, finally closing a loop between sea and land.

"一带一路"建设,有助于促进沿线各国经济繁荣与区域经济合作,促进世界和平发展。

The building of "One Belt One Road" could help promote the economic prosperity of the countries along its route and promote world peace through development.

"一带一路"战略的发力点在于通路、通航和通商,所有铁路、公路、口岸、银行、油气管道都将是建设或升级改造的重点。

The "One Belt One Road" initiative would focus on pathways, navigation and trade. Railways, highways, ports, banks, oil and gas pipelines would be the key points for construction or upgrading.

五 丝路文化 Silk Road Culture

"丝绸之路（Silk Road）"是由西方人命名的。1877年，德国地理学家李希霍芬在他写的《中国》一书中，首次使用"丝绸之路"一词，代替了曾经出现过的"玉石之路"、"佛教之路"等名称。

The term "Silk Road" was first coined by Westerners. In 1877, the German geographer, Mr. Leahy used the word "silk road" in his book *China* for the first time instead of "Jade Road" or "Buddhist Path."

丝绸之路大大促进了亚洲、欧洲和非洲地区经济、科技和文化的交流。它使整个世界丰富多彩。它联系中国、印度、希腊、埃及和巴比伦等文明古国。丝绸之路成为沿线国家和人民之间的桥梁和对话的窗口。

The Silk Road greatly promoted trade and the exchange of technology and culture among Asia, Europe and Africa. It made the whole world more interesting and eventful. It linked such ancient civilizations of China, India, Greece, Egypt and Babylonia. It was a bridge for contact and dialogue between states and peoples along the Silk Road.

丝路沿线国家所传播和衍生的文化则被称为"丝路文化"。

The culture along the Silk Road is known as the Silk Road

Culture.

千百年来"和平合作、开放包容、互学互鉴、互利共赢"的丝绸之路精神薪火相传，推进了人类文明进步。

For thousands of years, the Spirit of the Silk Road—"peace and cooperation, openness and inclusiveness, mutual learning and benefit"—has been passed from generation to generation. It promoted the progress of human civilization.

六　连云港港口 Lianyungang Port

连云港港具有悠久的航运发展史，其前身大浦港于 1905 年正式对外开放，现港址始建于 1933 年。

Lianyungang port has a long history of shipping. The former Dapu Port first opened in 1905 but was officially recognized in 1933.

连云港港北部有 6 公里长的连岛作天然屏障，南以云台山为依托，海峡有两公里宽，气候等自然条件优越，是一个终年不冻良港，也是我国八大海港之一。

There are six-kilometer-long islands on the north of Lianyungang, forming a natural barrier for the city. To its south lies Yuntai Mountain where the strait is two kilometers wide. With an excellent climate and other superior natural conditions, Liangyungang Port is an ice-free harbor all year round and one of the eight major seaports in China.

连云港港是中国中西部地区最便捷、最经济的出海口。连云港港各类专业化泊位齐备,最大泊位 30 万吨级,年吞吐能力超 2 亿吨。

Lianyungang Port is the most convenient and an economic estuary of China's central and western regions. Lianyungang port has all kinds of specialized berths. The biggest garages are 300,000 tons and have an annual transfer of over 200 million tons of goods.

2013 年 9 月 7 日,在中国国家主席习近平与哈萨克斯坦国总统纳扎尔巴耶夫共同见证下,连云港市与哈萨克斯坦国有铁路股份公司(简称哈国铁公司)签署中哈连云港过境货物运输通道及货物中转分拨基地项目合作及协作协议。连云港中哈物流场站项目由连云港港口集团与哈国铁公司下属的哈铁快运物流有限公司签署项目合资协议、合资合同及章程,成为"丝绸之路经济带"建设的首个实体平台。

On September 7, 2013, Chinese President Xi Jinping and the President of Kazakhstan, Nursultan Nazarbayev, signed collaboration agreements on transit goods and transportation access and cargo trans-shipment through Lianyungang port. It was a base project with Kazakhstan State-Owned Railway Corporation

（hereinafter referred to as the Kazakh National Railway Company）. Lianyungang Port Group signed a joint venture project agreement，contracts and articles of association with the Kazakhstan Railway Express logistics Co.，Ltd.，which is subordinated to the Kazakh National Railway Company. This became the first entity platform of the construction of the "Silk Road Economic Belt."

任务　Tasks

小组讨论　Group Work

① 一带一路是什么时间提出的?

When was "One Belt One Road" first proposed?

② 一带一路是在什么会议上提出来的?

In which conference was the "One Belt One Road" proposed?

③ 一带一路的中心线路图是什么?

What is the center route of "One Belt One Road"?

第二节　两汉文化

Unit Two　Culture of the Han Dynasty

徐州，简称徐，古称"彭城"，江苏省省辖市，是涵盖苏鲁豫皖 20 余个地级市的地理中心、经济中心。

徐州有 5 000 多年文明史，2 600 多年建城史，是江苏境内最早出现的城邑。三千多年前，全国疆域分为九州，徐州即为九州之一。

Xuzhou (Xu for short), with the nickname of Pengcheng, is a provincially administered city of Jiangsu Province. It is the geographical and economic center of over 20 cities in Jiangsu Province, Shandong Province, Henan Province and Anhui Province. With a civilization of over 5,000 years, Xuzhou was built 2,600 years ago and was the earliest city in Jiangsu Province. Xuzhou was one of the nine states of the country over 3,000 years ago.

① 秦朝（公元前221 年—公元前 207 年），是中国历史上一个极为重要的朝代，是由战国后期的秦国发展起来的中国历史上第一个大一统王朝。

The Qin Dynasty (221 B. C.—207 B. C.) was a very important dynasty in Chinese history. It was the first unified dynasty which developed from the Qin Kingdom at the end of the Warring States Period.

公元前 202 年，**汉朝继秦**①而兴，前后历 400 余年，经济、文化及国家的统一有了新的发展，原称华夏的中原居民称为汉人，其语言称为汉语，其文化学说称为汉学，也形成了中国乃至世界人口最多的一个民族——汉族。两汉指的是西汉与东汉，这是史学家们因其定都地点的不同而命名。

徐州是两汉文化的发源地，有"彭祖故国、刘邦故里、项羽故都"之称，两千年来汉文化的积淀和发展，使这里物华天宝、人杰地灵。徐州的两汉文化遗存十分丰富，其中的汉墓、汉画像石、汉俑并称为"汉代三绝"。

In 202 B. C.，the Han Dynasty was set up after the Qin Dynasty，and experienced new development in economy，culture and national unity over 400 years. Residents in Zhongyuan area were called Han people and their language was called Hanyu（Chinese）. Their culture was called sinology（Chinese studies），and the Han nationality began to grow，eventually becoming the largest population in China. The Han Dynasty refers to the Western and Eastern Han，due to the names historians gave the capitals in those areas.

Xuzhou is the birthplace of the Eastern Han and the Western Han，also the hometown of Emperor Liu Bang. With over 2,000 years of accumulation and development of the Han Culture，Xuzhou became a land of plenty with good products and outstanding talents. There are numerous historical relics of the Han Dynasty，among which the Han tombs，the Han Terra Cotta and the Han stone Carving are known as the "Three Perfections of the Han Dynasty."

 辉煌汉史 **The Splendid History of the Han Dynasty**

Emperor Gaozu of Han（Liu Bang）

汉朝分为"西汉"（公元前202年—公元9年）与"东汉"（公元25年—公元220年）两个历史时期，后世史学家亦称两汉。西汉为汉高祖刘邦（公元前256年—公元前195年）所建立，建都长安；东汉为汉光武帝刘秀（公元前5年—57年）所建立，建都洛阳。其间曾有王莽（公元前45年—公元23年）篡汉自立的短暂新朝（公元9年—公元23年）。

汉代是中国第二个大一统的王朝。它继承和巩固了秦朝开始的统一国家，经济繁荣，国力强盛、人民安乐，呈现出一派太平盛世的景象。在此期间，中国一直以世界强国的面目屹立于世界之林。

The Han Dynasty is divided into two historical periods，including the Western Han（202 B. C.—A. D. 9）and the Eastern Han（A. D. 25—A. D. 220）. Thus，the Han Dynasty as a whole was given by historians. Western Han Dynasty was established by Liu Bang，the Emperor Gaozu of Han，with the capital of Chang'an. The Eastern Han Dynasty was established by Liu Xiu，Emperor of Han Guangwu，with the capital of Luoyang. During the Han Dynasty，there was a short new dynasty named Xin（A. D. 9—A. D. 23），which was established by the former regent Wang Mang.

The Han Dynasty was the second dynasty to unify China. It inherited and consolidated the country after the Qin Dynasty. The Han Dynasty brought the country into economic prosperity and brought the people peace and happiness. During this period，China had a standing in the world as a strong country.

Map of Western Han

Map of Eastern Han

汉朝共 29 位皇帝，享国 405 年。汉文帝（公元前 202 年—公元前 157 年）、汉景帝（公元前 187 年—公元前 141 年）相继休养生息开创"文景之治"。汉武帝（公元前 156 年—公元前 87 年）即位后攘夷扩土，史称"汉武盛世"，至昭宣时期西汉国力达到极盛，史称"昭宣中兴"。光武帝刘秀确立与民休息的国策，开创了"光武中兴"。汉明帝（公元 28 年—公元 75 年）、汉章帝（57 年—88 年）沿袭轻徭薄赋开创明章之治。汉和帝（79 年—105 年）继位后开创"永元之隆"，东汉国力达到极盛。

There are a total of 29 emperors in the Han Dynasty over its 405 years. Emperor Wen of Han（B. C. 202—157）and Emperor Jing of Han（B. C. 187—141）recuperated and built up strength to create the Enlightened Administration of the Han Emperors Wen and Jing. After Emperor Wu of the Han Dynasty

(B. C. 156—87）ascended the throne，he expanded the land to create a Flouring Age of Wu. Until the Zhaoxuan period, the Western Han Dynasty was in its heyday, called Zhaoxuan Prosperity. Liu Xiu, Emperor Guangwu of Han, established a national policy to create Guangwu Prosperity. Emperors Ming and Zhang of the Han Dynasty followed the former emperors to create Mingzhang Control. Emperor He of the Han ascended the throne and created the Yongyuan Uplift. Thus, the Eastern Han Dynasty reached its peak.

二 璀璨文化 The Brilliant Culture of the Han Dynasty

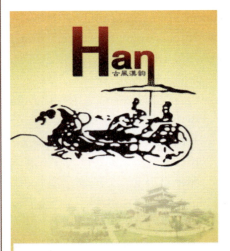

汉朝是中国发展史上的第一个黄金时期。受到华夏文化浸润的人民，在汉朝形成一个统一的民族——汉族。汉族后来成为世界上最大的民族。汉族在中国各兄弟民族中一直处于主导地位。其使用的语言称为汉语，形成的文字称为汉字，汉学也成为中国文化学说的主体部分，均延续至今。此外，还有遗留下来的汉服、汉乐、**汉赋**②等相关文化遗产。

② 汉赋是汉代涌现出的一种有韵的散文。

Han-fu was a kind of rhythmic prose in the Han Dynasty.

The Han Dynasty was a golden time in Chinese history. It formed the biggest nation-state to live on the broad land—Han People, with a unique cultural origin and integration. Since then, it became the basis for all the future nations, whose language was called Mandarin and whose character was called Chinese Characters. Thus sinologism became the body of Chinese culture from then on.

In addition，the Han-style clothes，music as well as poems were also passed down to its later generations.

汉武帝刘彻派遣**张骞**③出使西域，前后历时 13 年，最远到达了现在的中亚地区，开拓了后世闻名的"丝绸之路"，促进了中国与西域之间政治、经济、军事和文化的交流。

Emperor Wu of the Han Dynasty sent Zhang Qian to embark on a business trip to the western regions, which lasted 13 years. He reached as far away as Central Asia, and became known as the founder of the famous "Silk Road," which promoted the communication in politics, economics, military and culture.

③ 张骞（公元前 164 年—公元前 114 年）：中国汉代杰出的外交家、旅行家、探险家。

Zhang Qian (164B. C.—114B. C.) was an outstanding diplomat, traveler and explorer in the Han Dynasty.

公元 132 年,东汉科学家张衡发明了世界上第一台地震预测仪器——地动仪；蔡伦改进了造纸术，被列为**中国古代"四大发明"**④。

In 132 A. D., Zhang Heng, a scientist in Eastern Han, invented the first device in the world of Seismography, which could predict earthquakes. Cai Lun improved the papermaking technique. Both of these were listed in the "Four Greatest Inventions" of the ancient China.

汉武帝时，采纳**董仲舒**⑤"天人三策"、"愿陛下兴太学，置明师，以养天下之士"的建议，于京师长安设立太学，是汉代出现的设在京师的全国最高教育机构，为隋代国子监的前身。

Emperor Wu of the Han Dynasty adopted Dong Zhongshu's

④ 中国古代四大发明：造纸术、指南针、火药及活字印刷术。

Four Great Inventions include Papermaking, Compass, Gunpowder and Movable-type Printing.

⑤ 董仲舒（公元前 179 年—公元前 104 年）：汉代思想家、哲学家、政治家、教育家。

Dong Zhongshu (179 B. C.—104 B. C.) was a thinker, philosopher, politician and educator.

"Three Policies" to integrate heaven with the people. It emphasized higher education, expert cultivation and strict standards for the selection of the talents. Thus, the imperial college was set up in the capital city of Chang'an, which was the highest education institute at that time and was also the historical antecedent of the Imperial College in the Sui Dynasty.

中国汉族传统节日体系基本上在汉朝时期确立了下来；汉武帝在位时，确立了后世皇帝们的一种纪年方法——年号。

Chinese traditional festivals were established in the Han Dynasty. During the reign of Emperor Wu of the Han Dynasty, the reigning title was set as a calendar for the later emperors.

 多彩遗存——徐州的汉代遗存
Colorful Relics of Han Dynasty

⑥ 刘邦（公元前256—195），汉朝开国皇帝，建立了汉朝。

Emperor Liu Bang was the founding emperor of the Han Dynasty.

Tomb of Prince of Chu state

徐州是汉高祖**刘邦**⑥的故乡，两汉文化的发源地。两汉四百年间，徐州共有 13 位楚王、五个彭城王，应有 18 座王陵墓葬，合称"徐州汉代十八陵"。

Xuzhou is the hometown of Han Emperor Liu Bang and the birthplace of the Eastern Han and Western Han cultures. During 400 years of its reign, all 18 burial tombs (including tombs for thirteen Kings of the State of Chu and five Kings of Pengcheng) are located in Xuzhou, which is called the 18 Mausoleums of the Han Dynasty in Xuzhou.

徐州是汉代楚国的都城所在地，因而徐州市附近的山岗之上分布

Lion Hill Tomb

Beidongshan Tomb

Guishan Han Tomb

着许多楚王陵墓,其中较为著名的有楚王山、狮子山、北洞山、小龟山、东洞山、南洞山、卧牛山等。

Xuzhou is located in the capital of the State of Chu in the Han Dynasty. Around the area there were many Chu burial tombs, such as the famous Chu King Mountain, Lion King Mountain, Northern Hole Mountain, Little Turtle Mountain, Eastern Cave Mountain, South Cave Mountain, Crouched Ox Mountain, and so on.

位于徐州市南部的汉画像石艺术馆是一个集汉画像石雕刻、展览与研究为主题的展览馆。

As a special-subject gallery for the collection, the exhibition and research of Han stone sculptures, the Gallery of Stone Sculptures of the Han Dynasty is located in the southern suburb of Xuzhou.

汉兵马俑博物馆是一个建于1984年的文物博物馆,其馆藏有占地约10 000平方米的6条兵马俑坑。

The Museum of Terracotta Warriors and Horses of the Han Dynasty is a museum of relics excavated in 1984, housing six pits of Terracotta Warriors and Horses in an area

思考 Question

为什么在汉朝徐州这里的王称为"楚王"呢?

Why were the kings in Xuzhou called the Prince of the Chu State in the Han Dynasty?

思考 Question

你知道中国还有哪个城市也有兵马俑吗?

Do you know which other city also has Terracotta Warriors and Horses in China?

of some 10,000 square meters.

馆藏第一件物品就是被称为汉代三宝之一的 2 000 年前的兵马俑。这些兵马俑在六条俑坑中有序排列。前三条俑坑中是楚王的军事编队，第四条是警卫团，往西北 125 米处的第五与第六俑坑中的是由 200 马匹和骑兵组成的后备兵团。

The item you may visit first is one of the three treasures of the age, the Terracotta Horses and Warriors 2,000 years ago. Looking down on them you can see that they are distributed in the six pits. The first three pits contain the military formations of the Prince of Chu; in the fourth pit stand guard regiments; 125 meters to the northwest in the fifth and sixth pits are the reserve troops, made up of 200 terracotta horses and cavalrymen.

迄今为止，全国仅有三处已经挖掘出来的兵马俑，而徐州兵马俑的发现展示了西汉时期徐州这座城市的政治和军事强大实力。

So far only three sites of such Terracotta Warriors and Horses have been excavated in China, and the discovery of Xuzhou's shows the political and military significance of the city in the Western Han Dynasty.

  任务　Tasks

1. 单人活动　Individual Work

你的国家有哪些著名的古代陵墓？如果有，能不能介绍一下它的主人、年代和特点？

What are the ancient tombs in your home country?

Would you please introduce its owner，history and characteristics?

2. 单人活动　Individual Work

请将左边列表中的人物和右边列表中信息连起来。

Please match the names from the left with the information on the right.

张衡 Zhang Heng	文景之治 The Reign of the Empire Wen and Jing
汉武帝 Emperor Wu of Han	丝绸之路 The Silk Road
汉文帝与汉景帝 Emperor Wen of Han and Emperor Jing of Han	发明地动仪 Invented the First Seismograph
蔡伦 Cai Lun	光武中兴 Emperor Guangwu Revitalized the Han
张骞 Zhang Qian	改进造纸术 Improved Papermaking Technique
光武帝刘秀 Liu Xiu， Emperor Guangwu	汉武盛世 The Prosperity During the Reign of Emperor Wu

3. 小组活动　Group Work

看图，将表中对应的画像石内容或俑的名称填写到图片后的括号里。

Look at the pictures and fill in the names in the brackets from the table.

(　　)

(　　)

(　　)

(　　)

(　　)

(　　)

序号	名称
A	杂技俑 Acrobatics Figurines
B	击鼓说唱俑 Rap Drumming Figurines
C	表现旅行、外出的画像石 The Stone Sculpture of Journeys
D	舞蹈俑 Dancing Figurines
E	伎乐俑 Musician Figurines
F	表现农耕的画像石 The Stone Sculpture of Farming

第三篇　传统文化
Part Three　Traditional Culture

第一章　传统节日
Chapter One　Traditional Festivals

文化贴士9

中国的传统节日形式多样，内容丰富，是中华民族悠久历史文化的一个重要组成部分。节日的起源和发展是一个逐渐形成、潜移默化地完善、慢慢渗入社会生活的过程，是人类社会发展到一定阶段的产物。中国古代的节日，大多和天文、历法、数学以及节气有关。节气为节日的产生提供了前提条件。最早的风俗活动和原始崇拜、迷信禁忌有关；神话传奇故事为节日增添了几分浪漫色彩；宗教对节日有冲击与影响；一些历史人物被赋予永恒的纪念意义渗入节日；所有这些都融合在节日的内容里，使中国的节日有了深沉的历史感。在汉代，我国主要的传统节日就已经定型；到唐代，节日已经从原始祭拜、禁忌神秘的气氛中解放出来，转为娱乐礼仪型，成为真正的佳节良辰。

本章选择介绍了江苏省汉民族的一些重要的传统节日。我国是个多民族国家，各民族都有自己的文化习俗和不同的节日，例如傣族的泼水节、回族的开斋节、蒙古族的那达慕大会等，都值得我们去探究。

Chinese traditional festivals, rich in content and variety, are an important part of Chinese history and culture. The origin and development of the festivals are slowly trand gradually integrated into social life. They are the product of the social development. Most Chinese ancient festivals are linked with astronomy, calendar，mathematics and solar interpretations. Solar interpretation provides the prerequisite for the festival. The earliest customs activities are related to primitive worship and superstitious taboo; myths and legends add a bit of romantic color to the festivals. Religions also play an important role in the festivals; and some historical figures have been given the eternal memorial significance into the festival. All these are condensed into the content of the festivals today, which make Chinese festivals more historical. By the Han Dynasty, the traditional festivals had been finalized. In the Tang Dynasty, holidays changed from the original ideas of worship, taboos and mystery into entertainment and revelry.

In this chapter, we will introduce some major traditional festivals of the Han nationality in Jiangsu Province. China is a multi-ethnic country, and each ethnic group has its own cultural customs and festivals, such as the Water-Splashing Festival of the Dais, the Eid Festival of the Hui, "the Nadam" in Mongolia and so on. They are all worthy of exploring.

第一节　春　节
Unit One   Spring Festival

1912 年之前的三千多年,中国人一直使用农历纪年。在此之前,春节与元旦是指同一天——农历一月的第一天。**辛亥革命**①之后,中国开始正式使用公元纪年,将公历 1 月 1 日定为元旦,春节仍沿用农历纪年方式,这是中国人最重视的一个传统节日,因为它是一年之始。

春节的重要性在于它体现了古代"天人合一"的哲学思想,标志着人们思想观念中自然和春季的和谐统一及人类与自然的重要新开端。

For over 3,000 years leading up to 1912, Chinese life was ordered solely according to the lunar calendar. In ancient China, the Spring Festival and New Year's Day referred to the same day— the first day of the first lunar month. After the 1911 Revolution, however, China formally adopted the solar calendar and made January 1 New Year's Day, as distinct from the traditional lunar calendar "Spring Festival." But Chinese people have always regarded the Spring Festival as more significant and as being the true beginning of a new year.

The importance of the Spring Festival is that it embodies the ancient Chinese philosophy "harmony between human and nature." It symbolizes the harmony between nature and spring season, and a vital starting point for human and nature.

① 辛亥革命:是指发生于公元 1911 年至 1912 年初,旨在推翻清朝专制帝制,建立共和政体的全国性革命。

The 1911 Revolution occurred from 1911 to early 1912, which was a national revolution to overthrow the Qing Dynasty and set up the Republican Government.

 一　由来与传说 Origin and Legend

古代,农业是中国人民的经济支柱,纪年则规范农业生产。中国古人通过天文观测发现,地球围绕太阳转动的 12 个月中,它变换着的方位引起了气候的阶段性变化和农业季节的不同。随后人们就在地球轨道上指定了 24 个位置叫作**"24 节气"**②。每个节气都有一个名字,代表地球上与气象和物候相关的变化。例如"立春"意为春天的

② 24 节气：the 24 *jieqi* （Chinese solar terms）refers to：立春 the Beginning of Spring 雨水 Rain Water 惊蛰 the Waking of Insects 春分 the Spring Equinox 清明 Pure Brightness 谷雨 Grain Rain 立夏 the Beginning of Summer 小满 Grain Full 芒种 Grain in Ear 夏至 the Summer Solstice 小暑 Slight Heat 大暑 Great Heat 立秋 the Beginning of Autumn 处暑 the End of Heat 秋分 the Autumn Equinox 寒露 Cold Dew 霜降 Frost Descent 立冬 the Beginning of Winter 小雪 Slight Snow 大雪 Great Snow 冬至 the Winter Solstice 小寒 Slight Cold 大寒 Great Cold

开始。

In ancient times, agriculture was the economic mainstay of China and its people. The purpose of establishing a calendar was to regulate agricultural production. Chinese ancients discovered, through astronomical observation, that during the earth's 12-month orbit around the sun, its changing position gave rise to periodical changes in climate and thus distinctive farming seasons. They subsequently designated 24 positions within the earth's orbit, calling them the 24 *jieqi*. Each *jieqi* was given a name that signified the related meteorological and phonological changes on the earth. For example, *Lichun* means the beginning of spring.

汉代首次将春节的时间定在立春；数轮改革之后，最终决定将农历一月的第一天确定为春节，这一天一般在立春前后。

It was first decided during the Han Dynasty that *Lichun* should be the day to celebrate the Spring Festival. Later, after several rounds of reform, it was finally agreed that the first day of the first lunar month, which generally occurs around *Lichun*, should be Spring Festival.

过春节也称为"过年"。"年"是传说中一个邪恶的猛兽，赶走这个"年"也就意味着迎来了新的一年。

Celebrating Spring Festival was also named *Guonian*. *Nian*, which means year, was a vicious monster in legend. Driving away the *Nian* means ushering in a new year.

二 节日与活动 Festivals and Celebrations

传统的过年不仅仅是指正月初一这一天,而是指从农历十二月二十三到正月十五这一段时间。期间包括农历二十三祭灶节、大年三十除夕、正月初一春节、正月初五接财神日、正月十五元宵节等节日。

The traditional Spring Festival not only refers to the certain day which is the first day of the first lunar month, but also the period which is from 23rd of the 12th lunar month to the 15th day of the first lunar month next year. It includes the festival for offering sacrifices to the kitchen god on the 23rd, New Year's Eve on the 30th, the Spring Festival on the 1st, the festival for welcoming the god of wealth on the 5th, and the Lantern Festival on the 15th of Lunar January.

过年期间的庆祝活动很多。有祭灶神、除尘、办年货、做包子、打年糕、贴春联、吃年夜饭、放爆竹、守岁、包饺子、穿新衣、拜年、给压岁钱、舞龙舞狮、迎财神、看花灯、吃元宵等。所有活动都有独特的民俗含义,也都代表了古代中国人民祈盼丰收与和平的美好愿望。

There are many celebrations during the Spring Festival, such as offering sacrifices to the kitchen god, spring cleaning, Spring Festival shopping, making steamed buns and New Year pudding, putting up the couplets, having a special dinner on New Year's eve, setting off firecrackers, staying-up late on the eve of the festival, making dumplings, wearing new clothes, paying New Year's visits to friends, giving new year's lucky money, the dragon

思考 Question

1. "压岁钱"有什么含义?

What does new year's lucky money represent?

2. "放爆竹"的目的是什么?

What's the purpose of setting off firecrackers?

119

and lion dance，welcoming the god of wealth，watching the lanterns，eating *yuanxiao*，etc. Every event has its distinctive folk custom meaning，and symbolizes the hope of Chinese ancients for peace and harvests.

三　元宵节 The Lantern Festival

③ 元宵：由糯米制成，或实心，或带馅。馅有豆沙、白糖、山楂、各类果料等。人们以此怀念离别的亲人，寄托了对未来生活的美好愿望。

Yuanxiao are small dumpling balls made of glutinous rice flour with a filling of rose petals，sesame seeds，bean paste，jujube paste，crushed walnut，dried fruit，sugar and a little cooking oil. People eat them to denote union，harmony and happiness for the family.

　　元宵节③是春节的最后一天,标志着春节正式结束。正月十五是花灯(元宵)节,因为农历第一个月被称为元月(或者正月),而在古代夜晚又称"宵"。十五那天是一年中第一个圆月之日,所以那天又叫作圆宵节。

The Lantern Festival is on the last day of the Spring Festival. It also marks the official end of the Spring Festival. The 15th day of the 1st lunar month is the Chinese Lantern Festival because the first lunar month is called the *yuan* month. In the ancient times people called night *xiao*. The 15th day is the first night to see a full moon. So the day is also called Yuanxiao Festival in China.

　　根据中国传统,新年伊始,皓月当空,人们也能欣赏到满天的繁星。此时,人们举家在一片祥和的氛围中猜灯谜、看花灯和吃元宵。

According to the Chinese tradition，at the very beginning of a new year，when there is a bright full moon hanging in the sky，

there should be thousands of colorful lanterns hung out for people to appreciate. At this time，people will try to solve the puzzles on the lanterns，watch lanterns and eat *yuanxiao*（glutinous rice ball）. Families get together to celebrate the festival. Thus，it is also named the Latern Festival.

随着时间的推移,元宵节的活动越来越多,白天有耍龙灯、耍狮子、踩高跷、划旱船、扭秧歌、打太平鼓等传统民俗表演。到了夜晚,除了五颜六色的花灯之外,还有艳丽多姿的烟火。

In the daytime of the Lantern Festival，performances such as dragon lantern dance，lion dance，land boat dance，*yangge* dance，walking on stilts and beating drums while dancing will be staged. At night，there are not only magnificent lanterns，but also fireworks going off to create a vibrant night.

任务 Tasks

单人活动 Individual Work

读出以下这些春节习俗的名称。

Read the following customs in the Spring Festival.

放爆竹 **setting off firecrackers**

踩高跷 **walking on stilts**

贴春联 **putting up the couplets**

拜年 **paying New Year's visits**

第二节 清明节
Unit Two Qingming Festival

① 春分：时间一
般是在公历 3 月 20 日
或 21 日。
The Spring Equinox： March 20 or 21.

② 立夏：时间一
般是在公历 5 月 5 日
或 6 日。
The Beginning of Summer：May 5 or 6.

　　清明节,也称"扫墓节",是中国 24 节气之一,一般在公历 4 月 4 日或 5 日,位于**春分**①和**立夏**②之间。清明是中国传统节日,也是最重要的祭祀节日之一,是祭祖和扫墓的日子。2013 年,清明节被列入第一批国家级非物质文化遗产名录。

　　清明期间有扫墓、踏青、放风筝、插柳、荡秋千等民俗活动。这个节日既有慎终追远的感伤情怀,又有欢喜赏春的喜庆气氛。2008 年开始,"清明节"被列入法定节假日。

Qingming Festival，also known as "Pure Brightness Festival" or Tomb-Sweeping Day，is one of the 24 *jieqi* of the Chinese calendar. It normally falls on the 4th or 5th of April in the solar calendar，between the spring plowing and the summer weeding. It is a time to pay respects to one's ancestors and to tidy their gravesites. Qingming Festival was listed into the first group of national intangible cultural heritage in 2013.

Qingming Festival is a time of many different activities，among which the main ones are tomb sweeping，taking a spring outing and flying kites. Some other lost customs like planting willow trees and riding on swings have added infinite joy in past days. The festival is a combination of sadness and happiness，perhaps bittersweet. It has become a statutory public holiday since 2008.

 由来与传说 Origin and Legend

　　在二十四节气中,既是节气又是节日的只有清明。清明最早只是一种节气的名称,后变成纪念祖先的节日与寒食节有关。

Qingming Festival is the only holiday which is both a calendar

holiday and also one of the 24 *jieqi* in the Chinese traditional calendar. It was just a name of *Jieqi* and related to Hanshi Day but later became a day to worship the ancestors.

传说,寒食节是为了纪念介子推③。此人曾经在晋文公流亡期间帮助他渡过难关。晋文公即位之后介子推因故去世,为纪念他而定寒食节;而晋文公在寒食节之后一天前去祭拜,故而这一天被后人称为清明节。

It was said that Hanshi Day was set to be a memorial day for Jie Zitui. Jie Zitui helped Prince Jinwengong out when he was exiled abroad. After Prince Jinwengong ascended the throne, in order to remember Jie Zitui, Hanshi Day was set up. The day affer this day Jin Wengong went to worship him, therefore this day was later known as the Tomb Sweeping Day.

③ 介子推:逝于春秋时期的公元前636年。他是在晋文公即位之前的众多追随者之一。

Jie Zitui died in 636 B. C. in the Spring and Autumn Period. He was one of the followers of Prince Jinwengong before he became a duke.

清明扫墓始于后汉建武十年(公元34年),由光武帝提倡,至今已有两千年。最早,古人死后自然归于黄土,在宗庙留一个牌位祭祀。到秦始皇时才在墓侧加盖陵寝,汉代承袭。唐朝唐玄宗下诏开始扫墓。寒食上墓,随以为俗。

Tomb Sweeping Day began in the 10th year of Jianwu's reign (A. D. 34) in the Eastern Han Dynasty, which was advocated by Emperor Guangwu. In the ancient times, after people died, they were buried underground and a ritual tablet was left in the temple as commemoration. This tradition continued until Emperor Qin Shihuang began to build mausoleums by sides of the tombs. Emperor Xuanzong of the Tang Dynasty made the decision to sweep the tomb. Thus, it came about the tradition of sweeping the tomb on Hanshi Day.

清明节的名称与气候的特点有关。此时气温变暖,降雨增多,正是春耕春种的大好时节。所以清明对于古代农业生产而言是一个重要的节气。

Tomb Sweeping Day is closely related with the weather and climate. During this time of year, the weather gets warmer, rain increases, and it is the best time for plowing and sowing. So it was important for agricultural production in ancient times.

 习俗与活动 Customs and Activities

清明节最主要的习俗是扫墓,向死者表示尊重,体现了儒家的孝道思想。人们要根除亲人墓地周围的杂草、掸墓碑的灰尘、用鲜花装饰墓碑,还要摆放祭品和纸钱。

One major custom of Qingming Festival is tomb sweeping. It is meant to honor the dead, which is one of many ways that Confucians demonstrate filial piety. On this day, people would uproot weeds near the family gravesites, wipe the tombstones and decorate the tombstones with fresh flowers, and then set out offerings of food and paper money.

④ 踏青:春天时外出郊游,欣赏美景。
Spring Outing: People go out and appreciate the beautiful scenes of nature in spring.

三月清明,春回大地,生机勃勃,阳光明媚,正是外出郊游和欣赏大自然美景的好时机。**踏青**④这个习俗可以追溯至唐朝,历代延续直至今日。春游不仅增添乐趣也能强身健体。

Not only is it a day for commemorating the dead, it is also a festival for people to enjoy themselves. During March, everything in nature takes on a new look, as trees turn green, flowers blossom, and the sun shines brightly. It is time to go out and appreciate nature during the festival. This custom can be traced back to the Tang Dynasty and followed by each dynasty since then. Spring outing not only adds joy to life but also promote a healthy body and mind.

放风筝是清明时节人们所喜爱的活动。过去,有的人把风筝放上蓝天后,便剪断牵线,任凭清风把它们送往天涯海角,据说这样能除病消灾,给自己带来好运。

Flying kites is an activity favored by many people during the Qingming Festival. What makes flying kites during this festival so special is that people cut the string while the kite is in the sky to let it fly free. It is said this brings good luck and eliminates disease.

清明时柳枝用来插在门前并扫墓,俗称"插柳"。荡秋千也是清明节的传统习俗之一。这项活动不仅能增强体质,还能培养勇敢精神,至今仍被广大儿童所喜爱。

During the Qingming Festival, willow branches are hung on the door and used to sweep the tombs. Playing on the swing was another traditional custom in this festival. It can not only improve people's health but also cultivate the brave spirit. This activity is still loved by children today.

任务 Tasks

小组活动 Group Work

先阅读下面这首古诗《清明》,然后小组讨论它的含义。
Read the following poem and discuss the meanings in groups.

清明

（唐·杜牧）

清明时节雨纷纷，
路上行人欲断魂。
借问酒家何处有，
牧童遥指杏花村。

Tomb Sweeping Day

Du Mu

It drizzles endless during the rainy season in spring,

Travelers along the road look gloomy and miserable.

When I ask a shepherd boy where I can find a tavern,

He points at a distant hamlet nestling amidst apricot blossoms.

（Yang Xianyi and Gladys Yang，Trans.）

第三节 端午节

Unit Three The Dragon Boat Festival

端午节（农历五月初五），也称龙舟节、双五节。端午节与春节、中秋节并列为中国三大传统节日，端午节是其中最古老的节日。早在吴越之地春秋之前就有在农历五月初五以龙舟竞渡形式举行部落图腾祭祀的习俗，后为纪念屈原的传统节日，也为祛病防疫的节日，部分地区也有纪念伍子胥、曹娥等说法。

端午节以吃粽子和赛龙舟为特色。2008 年，端午节被正式确定为公共假日。许多东亚国家也同样在该天举行庆祝活动。

The Dragon Boat Festival, also called the Duanwu Festival or Double Fifth Festival，is celebrated on the fifth day of the fifth month according to the Chinese lunar calendar. It is one of the three major Chinese festivals，along with the Spring Festival and the Mid-Autumn Festival. Of the three, the Dragon Boat Festival is possibly the oldest. Before the Spring and Autumn Period there were dragon boat races and the custom of tribal totem worship held on the fifth day of the fifth lunar month in Wu and Yue areas. Later，it developed into a festival to commemorate Qu Yuan. It is also a festival against epidemic illnesses，and in some areas it is also to commemorate Wu Zixu and Cao E.

For thousands of years，the festival has been marked by eating *Zongzi* and racing dragon boats. In 2008，the Dragon Boat Festival was restored in China as an official national holiday. The Dragon Boat Festival is a traditional and statutory holiday associated with Chinese culture，and it is celebrated in other East Asian countries as well.

一 由来与传说 Origin and Legend

传说公元前 278 年,屈原① 得知他的祖国被邻国侵略即将灭亡,悲愤交加,怀石自沉于汨罗江,以身殉国。汨罗江畔的居民为了挽救他们爱戴的屈原,划船在江内寻找,把鱼儿和邪灵从他尸体边赶走,又将用粽叶包好的米丢入汨罗江以驱赶江里的龙。

In 278 B.C., hearing the news that his home was perished by a neighboring state, Qu Yuan was said to jump into the Miluo River (in today's Hunan Province) with a great rock to commit suicide as an action to protest against the corruption of the era. Because of the respect to Qu Yuan, local people along the Miluo River rushed into their boats to search for him and tried to keep the fish and evil spirits from his body by throwing rice wrapped in leaves into the water to ward off the river dragons.

另一种说法是,农历五月天气湿热,人易生病,瘟疫也易流行。随着时代变迁,原先端午节的纪念意义逐渐向避邪驱瘟上转变。

Another belief is that because the humidity started to increase in May, people became easily to get sick at this time, so the festival also played a role in driving away the evil and disease. As time went by, the festival turned into a time for protecting from the evil and disease.

二 习俗与活动 Customs and Activities

赛龙舟是端午节最重要的活动,它体现了人们营救屈原的努力。在当代,龙舟竞赛也展示了合作与团队精神。

The most important activity in this festival is the Dragon Boat

① 屈原(公元前 340 年—公元前 278 年):屈原是中国历史上第一位伟大的爱国诗人,中国浪漫主义文学的奠基人,也是楚国重要的政治家。

Qu Yuan(340B. C.—278B. C.)is the first great patriotic poet of China, and he was the founder of romantic literature in China and was an important politician of the Chu State.

Races. They symbolize people's attempts to rescue Qu Yuan. In the current period, these races also demonstrate the virtues of cooperation and teamwork.

此外，端午节也以吃糯米粽子为标志。粽子是由竹叶或粽叶包裹，里面塞满混有不同馅料的糯米制成。

The festival has also been marked by eating *zongzi* (glutinous rice, or "rice cake"). *Zongzi* is made of glutinous rice stuffed with different fillings and wrapped in bamboo or reed leaves.

端午节，人们会在自家门口放艾草来去除房屋的霉运。

People will hang healthy herbs on the front door to clear the bad luck out of the house.

还有一个习俗便是涂饮雄黄酒，据说是可以避邪驱瘟，其实也可以起到驱虫的效果。

Another custom is to sprinkle and drink rice wine, which is said to drive away evil spirits. Actually, it can play a role in repelling insects.

在端午节时挂**钟馗**②画像是用来吓走鬼怪。

Hanging Zhong Kui's portrait during the Dragon Boat Festival is used to scare away ghosts.

② 钟馗：中国民间传说中能打鬼驱除邪祟的神，端午时能斩五毒。

Zhong Kui is the god who can dispel evil ghosts in Chinese folklore and eliminate "five poisons."

任务 Tasks

1. 单人活动 Individual Work

看图，将表中习俗活动的名称填写到图片下面的括号里

Look at the pictures and fill the names in the brackets from the table.

(　　)　　　　　　　　　(　　)　　　　　　　　　(　　)

序号 No.	习俗名称 Customs
A	悬艾草菖蒲 Hang Healthy Herbs
B	赛龙舟 the Dragon Boat Races
C	包粽子 Making *Zongzi*

2. 小组活动 Group Work

你的国家有没有一些类似端午节的活动？这些活动是如何开展的？

Do you know any similar festival as the Dragon Boat Festival in your own country? If YES，please talk about and discuss about how it is celebrated.

活动名称：
Name of Activities：_____
国家：
Country：_____
具体活动：
Details：_____

第四节   中秋节

Unit Four   The Mid-Autumn Festival

中秋节,又称拜月节或团圆节,是中华民族的传统文化节日,时间在农历八月十五;因其恰值**三秋之半**①,故名中秋节。中秋节始于唐朝初年,盛行于宋朝,至明清时,已成为与春节齐名的中国主要节日之一。

受中华文化的影响,中秋节也是东亚和东南亚一些国家尤其是当地华人华侨的传统节日。自2008年起中秋节被列为国家**法定节假日**②。

中秋节以月之圆兆人之团圆,为寄托思念故乡,思念亲人之情,祈盼丰收、幸福,成为丰富多彩、弥足珍贵的文化遗产。

The Mid-Autumn Festival,which is also known as Baiyue Festival or the Gathering Holiday,is celebrated on the 15th day of the 8th month of the lunar calendar. In China,the lunar calendar is divided quarterly into Meng,Zhong and Ji,so the Mid-Autumn Festival is also called Zhongqiu. The holiday originated from the early Tang Dynasty and flourished in the Song Dynasty. It was one of the most important Chinese festivals in the Ming and Qing Dynasties.

Influenced by Chinese culture,the Mid-Autumn Festival is a traditional festival in East and Southeast Asia,especially for the local Chinese and overseas Chinese there. Since 2008,the Mid-Autumn Festival has been listed as a national official holiday.

The Mid-Autumn Festival is a time for family reunion and missing one's hometown and their loved ones. It prays for a good harvest and happiness. It has become a rich and precious cultural heritage.

① 三秋之半:阴历七月、八月、九月为秋季。七月称孟秋;八月称仲秋;九月称季秋。统称三秋。三秋之半即仲秋之半。

The Quarterly calendar is divided into Meng,Zhong and Ji,so the Mid-Autumn Festival is also called Zhongqiu.

② 中国的国家法定节假日包括元旦、春节、清明节、五一节、端午节、国庆节和中秋节。

Chinese official holidays include:New Year's Day,Spring Festival,Qingming Festival,May Day,Dragon Boat Festival,National Day and Mid-Autumn Festival.

 由来与传说 Origin and Legend

关于中秋节的起源，说法较多。一是起源于古代帝王的祭祀活动。早在春秋时期，帝王就已开始祭月、拜月了。后来贵族官吏和文人学士也相继效仿，逐步传到民间。

The origins of the Mid-Autumn Festival vary a lot. One statement is that it originated from imperial sacrificial activities in ancient China. As early as the Spring and Autumn Period, the emperor began to worship the moon. Later, noble officials and literates had to follow. Eventually, this practice began to spread among people.

二是中秋节的起源和农业生产有关。秋天是收获的季节。八月中秋，农作物和各种果品陆续成熟，农民为了庆祝丰收，表达喜悦的心情，就以"中秋"这天作为节日。

The other statement is that the festival is related to agricultural production. Autumn is the harvest season. The festival is thought to be set up in order to celebrate the harvest of various fruits and crops, and to express their gratitude to the bountiful harvest.

③嫦娥：中国古代神话中的仙女，神射手后羿的妻子，住在月亮上的月宫中，怀中经常抱着一只玉兔。

Chang-E, who is the strong archer Hou Yi's wife, is well known as a fairy in ancient Chinese myths and legends. She lives in the moon with a rabbit in her arms.

此外，**嫦娥**③奔月的神话故事赋予了中秋节神话色彩。传说远古时期，天空曾有 10 个太阳，一天，10 个太阳同时出现，酷热难挡。神射手后羿射下其中9个,拯救了生灵。天帝赏赐给他两份长生不老药,却被她的妻子嫦娥全部偷偷喝下,结果就飞向了离地面最近的月宫。

The festival was later given a mythological flavor with legends of Chang-E, the beautiful lady in the moon. According to Chinese mythology, the earth once had 10 suns circling over it. One day, all 10 suns appeared together, scorching the earth with their heat. The archer Yi shot down nine of them, leaving just one sun, and was given the elixir of immortality as a reward. However, his wife Chang-E drank herself and flew upwards towards the heavens, choosing the moon as residence.

习俗与活动 Customs and Activities

自周代开始,每逢中秋夜都要举行迎寒和祭月。设香案、摆祭品,全家人依次拜祭月亮,并按全家人数切好**月饼**④。唐宋明清时期,中秋赏月十分盛行。每逢这一日,"贵家结饰台榭,民间争占酒楼玩月"。直至今日,一家人围坐在一起,欣赏皓月当空的美景仍是中秋佳节必不可少的活动之一。

Since the beginning of the Zhou Dynasty, welcoming coldness through worship of the moon was held during the mid-autumn night. The whole family followed to worship the moon by placing offerings on a special table and shared moon cakes. In the Tang, Song, Ming and Qing Dynasties, to celebrate the Mid-Autumn Festival was very popular. No matter the rich or the poor, people celebrated the festival

④ 月饼:久负盛名的汉族传统小吃,面皮由面粉、酥油和糖制成,内馅有豆沙、五仁、莲蓉等种类。

Moon cake is the famous Chinese traditional snack. It is made of flour, butter and sugar with a filling made of red bean paste, five kernels and Lianrong, etc.

by decorating the house or going out to a restaurant together. Even today, it is still necessary for families to gather to appreciate the moon in the sky during the Mid-Autumn Festival.

中秋节吃月饼是中国各地过中秋节的必备习俗,人们把赏月与月饼结合在一起,寓意家人团圆,寄托思念。

Eating moon cakes is a necessary custom in the Mid-Autumn Festival throughout China. People enjoy the full moon while eating moon cakes to symbolize family reunion.

中秋之夜,仰望着月中丹桂,闻着阵阵桂香,喝一杯桂花蜜酒,欢庆合家甜甜蜜蜜,已成为节日一种美的享受。

On the night of the Mid-Autumn Festival, looking up at the moon in the sky, smelling the osmanthus and drinking a cup of sweet scented osmanthus wine have become a great joy for families.

任务　Tasks

1. 单人活动　Individual Work

看图,将列表中的信息与图片连起来。

Look at the pictures and match the information in each table.

后羿射日
Archer Yi shoots down nine suns

嫦娥奔月
Chang-E flies to the moon

吴刚伐桂
Wu Gang cuts the laural

2. 小组活动　Group Work

中国古代不少诗人在中秋赏月时吟诵出许多与月亮有关的诗句,例句如下。请与小组成员一起找类似的诗句,比赛谁找得最多。

Many poets in ancient China recite many verses associated with the moon in the Mid-Autumn Festival，as you can see in the following examples. Please find them with your group members and compete with each other.

例如:① 海上生明月,天涯共此时。

Over the sea the moon shines bright；we gaze at it far，far apart.

② 但愿人长久,千里共婵娟。

May we all be blessed with longevity. Though far apart，we are still able to share the beauty of the moon together.

你找到的诗句有 The verses you find are as follows：

文化贴士10

第二章　传统饮食
Chapter Two　Traditional Cuisine

中国饮食文化历史源远流长,博大精深,在几千年的历史长河中,已成为中国传统文化的一个重要组成部分。中国饮食文化主要有风味多样、四季有别、讲究美感、注重情趣和食医结合五个主要特点。

中国传统饮食文化主要包括菜系风味流派、茶文化、酒文化等。中国的传统菜系主要包括巴蜀、齐鲁、淮扬、粤闽四大菜系。中国是茶的故乡,是世界上最早发现茶树、利用茶叶和栽培茶树的国家。中国茶的种类按照茶叶的种类来分,有绿茶、黑茶、黄茶、青茶、红茶、白茶,以及经过熏制的花茶。中国制酒历史悠久,品种繁多,名酒荟萃,享誉中外。酒渗透于整个中华五千年的文明史中,从文学艺术创作、文化娱乐到饮食烹饪、养生保健等各方面在中国人生活中都占有重要的位置。

China is an ancient civilization with a broad and profound traditional food culture. After several thousand years' refinement, Chinese food culture has formed unique characteristics and become an important part of Chinese traditional culture. There are five main characteristics of Chinese cuisine, various flavors, seasonal variation, aesthetic feeling, sense of interest and combination of health and medicine.

Chinese traditional food culture mainly includes cuisine styles, tea culture and wine culture, etc. Traditional Chinese cuisine mainly includes four flavors: Bashu, Qilu, Huaiyang and Yuemin Cuisines. China is the land of tea, and was the first country to discover Chinese tea trees, to make use of Chinese tea-leaves and plant trees. According to the type of tea-leaves, it could be divided into green tea, black tea, oolong tea, yellow tea, black tea, white tea and scented tea. Wine is one of the other main beverages in human life. Chinese wine has a long history, great varieties, and enjoys enormous popularity throughout the world. Wine has been important throughout all of the Chinese civilization of 5,000 years. It plays an important role in Chinese people's lives, from the literary and artistic to the cultural entertainment and cooking. It's even important in traditional Chinese health care.

第一节　传统菜系分类

Unit One　Types of Traditional Cuisine

菜系，也称帮菜，是指在选料、切配、烹饪等技艺方面，经长期演变而自成体系，具有鲜明的地方风味特色，并为社会所公认的中国饮食的菜肴流派。

中国幅员辽阔，地大物博，各地气候、物产、风俗习惯都存在差异。早在春秋战国时期，中国南北菜肴风味就表现出差异。中国一直就有"南米北面"的说法，口味上有"南甜北咸东酸西辣"之分，主要是鲁菜、川菜、粤菜和淮扬菜为传统"四大菜系"，后加上浙菜、闽菜、徽菜、湘菜则被称为"八大菜系"。

Cuisine，also called Bangcai，refers to the material，cutting and cooking skills，which evolves over a long period of time and has given rise to their own system with distinctive local flavors unique to the country.

China has a vast territory and abundant resources. The climate，products and customs of each area are different. In early years，during the Spring and Autumn Period and the Warring States Period，northern and southern cuisines in Chinese food culture first began to show differences. China has an old saying "Nan Mi Bei Mian" and has "south sweet，north salty，east sour，west spicy" tastes. Shandong Cuisine，Sichuan Cuisine，Cantonese Cuisine and the Huaiyang Cuisine are the main traditional "Four Major Cuisines，" and then adding the less known Zhejiang Cuisine，Fujian Cuisine，Anhui Cuisine and Hunan Cuisine，to be called the "Eight Cuisines. "

① 自发型菜系：其基本技法土生土长，代代相传。

Spontaneous cuisine：It refers to cooking skills belonging to a local place and being handed down from generation to generation.

 鲁菜 Shandong Cuisine

鲁菜，也称山东菜，鲁菜是四大菜系中唯一的**自发型菜系**①。

Lu Cuisine，also called Shandong Cuisine，which is the only "spontaneous cuisine" among the four major cuisines.

鲁菜在中国北方享有很高的声誉，是北方菜的代表，影响遍及华北、东北等地。鲁菜的形成与发展，是由山东的文化、历史、地理环境、经济条件和世俗风尚所决定的。

Shandong Cuisine enjoys a high reputation in Northern China and it's the representative of northern cuisine. The formation and development of Shandong Cuisine is affected by culture，history，geography，economic conditions and the secular fashion of Shandong.

山东是我国古代文化的发祥地之一，位于黄河下游，黄河流域孕育了鲁菜。山东的粮食产量、水果产量、水产品产量都位居全国前列，丰富的物产为发展山东烹饪事业提供了取之不尽的物质资源。

Shandong is one of the birthplaces of China's ancient culture. It is located in the lower reaches of the Yellow River，where Shandong Cuisine originated. The output of grain，fruit and aquatic products in Shandong rank top in China. Rich natural resources are provided inexhaustible resources for the development of Shandong Cuisine.

九转大肠 Braised Intestines in Brown Sauce

一品肉 Yipin Meat

糖醋鲤鱼 Sweet-and-Sour Carp

清油盘丝饼 Fried Disc Cakes

川菜 Sichuan Cuisine

鱼香肉丝 **Shredded Meat in Chili Sauce**

宫保鸡丁 **Spicy Diced Chicken with Peanuts**

夫妻肺片 **Pork Lungs in Chili Sauce**

川菜即四川地区的菜肴，是最有特色的菜系，民间最大菜系，同时被冠以"百姓菜"。

Sichuan Cuisine is the food in Sichuan area. It's the most distinctive and the largest folk cuisine, also known as "commoner food."

川菜以麻、辣、鲜、香扬名海内外。川菜的风格朴实而又清新，具有浓厚的乡土气息。在国际上享有"食在中国，味在四川"的美誉。

Sichuan Cuisine is known for its hemp, with a spicy, fresh and fragrant aroma. The style of Sichuan Cuisine is simple and fresh, with a strong local flavor. It is popular around the world and regarded locally with the saying "Fresh in China, Flavor in Sichuan."

川菜中六大名菜是：鱼香肉丝、宫保鸡丁、夫妻肺片、麻婆豆腐、回锅肉、东坡肘子。

The most famous dishes of Sichuan Cuisine are：Shredded Meat in Chili Sauce，Spicy Diced Chicken with Peanuts，Pork Lungs in Chili Sauce，Stir-Fried Tofu in Hot Sauce，Double-Cooked Pork，and Dongpo Pig Knuckle.

麻婆豆腐 Stir-Fried Tofu in Hot Sauce

回锅肉 Double-Cooked Pork

 粤菜 Cantonese Cuisine

白切鸡
White Sliced Chicken

潮州卤水鸭
Chaoshan-Style Duck

脆皮乳猪
Roast Piglet with Crisp Skin

粤菜即广东菜，发源于岭南，以潮州菜为代表。粤菜对原料只是稍作处理，通过恰当地烹饪和调料来展现食物的原味。

Cantonese Cuisine, also called Guangdong Cuisine, originated in Lingnan and is represented by Chaozhou Cuisine. In Cantonese Cuisine, ingredients are usually prepared with a lighter seasoning, properly cooked and seasoned to bring out the natural flavors of the food.

粤菜中，海鲜菜肴最为有名，尤其是各式的蒸鱼和蒸贝类。粤菜著名的菜点有脆皮乳猪、鱼丸面、潮州卤水鸭等。

Cantonese Cuisine is famous for its seafood, especially steamed fish and shellfish prepared in various ways. Other typical dishes include Roast Piglet with Crispy Skin, Fishball Noodle Soup, and Chaoshan-Style Duck.

鱼丸面
Fishball Noodle Soup

粤菜是起步较晚的菜系,但它影响深远。世界各国的中餐馆,多数是以粤菜为主。在世界各地,粤菜与法国大餐齐名。因此,有不少人认为粤菜是海外中国的代表菜系。

Cantonese Cuisine started late, but it came to have a far-reaching influence. Chinese restaurants around the world are mainly Cantonese Cuisine restaurants. Cantonese Cuisine is as famous as French Cuisine around the world. So a lot of people think that Cantonese cuisine is what "Chinese food" tastes like.

四 淮扬菜 Huaiyang Cuisine

大煮干丝
Yangzhou Steamed Jerky Strips

清炖蟹粉狮子头
Stewed Meatballs with Crab

淮扬菜是以明清时期淮安府和扬州府为中心的淮扬地域性菜系,形成于淮安、扬州、镇江等地区,覆盖周围的泰州、盐城、南通等地,也是明清时期淮扬两府之辖地。

Originated from Huai'an and Yangzhou States in the Ming and Qing Dynasties, Huaiyang cuisine is formed in Huai'an, Yangzhou, Zhenjiang and other regions, covering Taizhou, Yancheng and Nantong, which were also under the jurisdiction of the two states at that time.

淮扬菜素有东南第一佳味、天下之致美的声誉。淮扬菜选材严谨,做工讲究,造型精美,味兼南北,追求本味,文化韵味十足。

Huaiyang Cuisine is known as the first delicacy in the

三套鸭
Triple Combo Duck

扬州炒饭
Yangzhou Fried Rice

southeast and has a good reputation around the world. Huaiyang Cuisine is characterized by rigorous, exquisite workmanship and style with both north and south flavors.

淮扬菜著名菜肴有扬州炒饭、清炖蟹粉狮子头、大煮干丝、水晶肉、三套鸭等。

The most famous dishes of Huaiyang Cuisine are Yangzhou Fried Rice, Stewed Meatballs with Crab, Yangzhou Steamed Jerky Strips, Crystal Meat and Triple Combo Duck.

淮扬菜亮相于 1949 年中华人民共和国开国大典首次国宴，史称"开国第一宴"。

Huaiyang Cuisine appeared on the founding ceremony of the People's Republic of China in 1949, known as "the first state banquet of China."

任务   Tasks

1. 小组活动   Group Work

看图，将列表中的信息与图片连起来。

Look at the pictures and match the information in each table.

据说在光绪三十二年（1906 年）兴起。原用红腐乳作调料，把肉烧成红腐乳大小，借用红腐乳的形与色，故名。

It's said that it was cooked in the 32nd year of the reign of Guangxu. Fermented red beancurd was originally used as seasoning, and meat was cut up to be the same size as the fermented red beancurd，thus named.

兴于 1872—1909 年（清光绪年间），其色泽酱红，肉质酥烂，骨香浓郁，汁浓味鲜，咸中带甜。

Prospering between 1872 and 1909（the reign of Guangxu of the Qing Dynasty），with a garnet red color，tender meat，rich flavor，juicy taste，fresh，salty and sweet.

相传是一个叫化子制作，将鸡去除内脏，带毛涂上泥巴，放入火中煨烤，待泥干成熟，敲去泥壳，鸡毛随壳而脱，香气四溢。

It's said that it was cooked by a beggar. He discarded a chicken's intestines, pasted mud without plucking its feathers, made it baked on fire, and then removed the cover of mud until it was dry. The feathers came off with the mud and the chicken smelt nice.

主要以虾仁为主料，巧用碧螺春作配料，成菜具有茶香味鲜、清淡爽口、色泽素雅。

Its basic ingredient is shrimp meat，adding some Biluochun. The dishes both have a light tea aroma and taste fresh and light with an elegant color.

2. 单人活动　Individual Work

介绍一下自己国家的美食。

Please talk about the cuisine in your own country.

第二节 传统酒文化
Unit Two Traditional Wine Culture

中国酿酒最初起源于夏初或夏朝以前的时期，距今已经有四千余年的历史。中国的茅台、五粮液、汾酒、竹叶青、泸州老窖、古井贡酒、加饭酒、张裕葡萄酒、长城干红葡萄酒等，都是享誉世界的名酒。

中国是酒的王国。酒，形态万千，色泽纷呈，品种之多，产量之丰，堪称世界之冠。中国又是饮酒人的乐土，地无分南北，人无分男女，饮酒之风，历经数千年而不衰。

Chinese liquor originated in the Xia Dynasty or the period before. It has more than four thousand years of history. A lot of famous Chinese liquors are known throughout the world，such as Maotai，Wuliangye，Fenjiu，Trimeresurus Stejnegeri，Luzhou Laojiao，the Gujing Distillery，Rice Wine，Zhangyu Wine，and Great Wall Dry Red Wine.

China is a kingdom of wine. There are various forms，brilliant colors，abundant varieties and a rich production. China is also a drinkers' paradise. People in both Northern and Southern regions，men and women alike enjoy a good drink of wine in China. The vogue of drinking wine has lasted for thousands of years and surely will last forever.

 酒的起源 The Origin of the Wine

中国人的祖先放弃了他们的游牧生活，选择在黄河流域群居时，种植了多种多样的谷物，这为日后酿造美酒奠定了基础。

When the primitive ancestors of Chinese people gave up their nomadic lifestyle and opted to live in communities in the Yellow River Valley，the plantation of various kinds of grain laid the foundation for making liquor.

仪狄和杜康被认为是中国造酒业的鼻祖。据史料记载,仪狄应君主禹的要求,付出了巨大的努力,终于成功地用发酵的糯米造出了芳醇的美酒。仪狄酿的酒很好喝,她把这一佳酒献给禹,希望能够得到奖赏。禹品尝过后,对此酒无与伦比的味道非常满意。然而,禹非但没有奖赏仪狄反而疏远了她。在这位帝王看来,酒充满诱惑,是邪恶的,担心因为过量饮酒会乱心智、损害国家。

Yidi and Dukang are considered to be two pioneers of the industry of making liquor. According to historical records, it was Yidi who first made great efforts to make liquor with fermented glutinous rice at the order of the Emperor Yu. The liquor made by Yidi tasted good. She presented the top-notch liquor to Emperor Yu, hoping to receive rewards. After tasting the liquor, Yu was satisfied with its unparalleled taste. However, the monarch did not reward her for her efforts, he even cut all communication with her. This was because in the eyes of the monarch, the mesmerizing liquor was wicked. He feared that indulging in excessive drinking could make him lose his wisdom and do something harmful to his country.

生活在夏朝的杜康,凭借用高粱米酿出美酒,而受到赞誉。据史书记载,冬日里一天,杜康将一些煮过的高粱米放进了树洞。第二年春天,从这个树洞中散发出浓郁的香味,扑鼻而入。之后,杜康发现正是发酵的高粱米散发出诱人的香气。这个偶然的发现给了他灵感。

Du Kang, living in the Xia Dynasty, also credited with making top-notch liquor with Chinese sorghum. According to historical legends, Du Kang stored some cooked Chinese sorghum seeds inside a hollow tree stump on a winter day. In the spring of the following years, a fragrant aroma wafted from the tree stump into Du Kang's nostrils. Afterwards, Du Kang found that it was the fermented sorghum seeds which gave off the alluring fragrance. This accidental discovery gave rise to his inspiration to make liquor with fermented sorghum seeds.

 酒文化 Chinese Wine Culture

酒文化的核心是"酒民文化"。酒广泛地融入了人们的生活,贴近"生活"的酒文化得到了空前的丰富和发展。相关的酒俗、酒礼成为了人们一项重要的生活内容。

The core of wine culture is the "Drinkers' Culture." Wine is widely integrated into people's lives. The extent to which wine culture has become intertwined with life is reaching unprecedented heights. Some related wine customs and ceremonies have become an important content of people's life.

中国的酒文化实则是一种社会文化。与中国人打交道，无论在怎样的场合，真正的饮酒，需要表达的也多是精神层面的内容——客从远方来，无酒不足以表达深情厚意；良辰佳节，无酒不足以显示欢快惬意；丧葬忌日，无酒不足以致其哀伤肠断；蹉跎困顿，无酒不足以消除寂寥忧伤；春风得意，无酒不足以抒发豪情壮志。

China's wine culture is a social culture. When interacting with Chinese people, no matter in what occasion, drinking is the most common and sincere way to express the spiritual happiness—a meeting without wine may lack kindness when meeting guests from afar; without wine there is no way to fully convey the merriment during festivals. Even at funerals, wine is necessary to express the sorrow and heartbreak of death. Without wine, one cannot sufficiently eliminate loneliness and sadness, nor can one fully express joy and celebration.

三 白酒香味解析 Types of White Wine

白酒酿制时由于原材料、加工工艺以及所处的环境气候不同，各个地区所酿制的酒品，其香韵特点也各不一样。主要有以下几类：

Due to the different raw materials, processing technology, environment and climate, the liquor brewed in various regions has

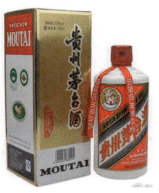

its own characteristics and fragrance, mainly including the following categories.

一是酱香型，又称茅香型，以贵州省仁怀市的茅台酒为典型代表。这种香型的白酒，以高粱为原料，一年一周期，二次投料，八次发酵，以酒养糟，七次高温烤酒，多次取酒，长期陈贮的酿造工艺酿制而成。

The first is Jiang-flavor, also known as Mao-flavor. Renhuai Maotai liquor in Guizhou Province is the typical representative. The scent of liquor comes from the sorghum it was made from. It has an annual cycle requiring two "feedings," and eight fermentation cycles. It needs to be boiled at a high temperature eight times before being bottled and stored for proper aging.

二是清香型，又称汾香型，以山西省汾阳市杏花村的汾酒为典型代表。这种香型的白酒以高粱等谷物为原料，采用清蒸清糟酿造工艺、固态地缸发酵、清蒸流酒，强调"清蒸排杂、清洁卫生"，即都在一个"清"字上下功夫，"一清到底"。

The second has a milder, more aromatic flavor, also known as Fen-flavor. Fen-wine comes from Xinghua village, Fenyang City, Shanxi Province. The scent of liquor also comes form its sorghum grains. It has been adapted from steam distillery soluble technology. It ferments for a long time in its solid state in a large cylinder. Then it is boiled out and the steam is collected as the final product. This leaves the wine with a "clear and clean" flavor.

三是浓香型，又称泸香型、窖香型。以四川泸州老窖特曲酒为典型代表。发酵原料以高粱为主，主要成分以乙酸乙酯为主体，以浓香甘爽为特点，发酵采用混蒸续渣工艺。

The third has a strong-flavor，also known as Lu-flavor or pit flavor. Luzhou Laojiao is a special liquor in Sichuan. It uses sorghum grains and caproic acid ethyl ester as the main ingredients. Its fresh and zesty aroma comes from its mixed steaming slag process.

四是米香型，以广西壮族自治区桂林市的三花酒为典型代表。这种香型的白酒以大米为主要原料，不加辅料，采用固态糖化、液态发酵、液态蒸馏、取酒贮存的工艺酿制而成。

The fourth is made of rice. Sanhua Wine in Guilin，Guangxi Zhuang Autonomous Region，uses rice as raw materials. It's made without adding supplementary materials，but using solid scarification during its liquid state fermentation，and then left to store for a long time.

五是凤香型，以陕西凤翔的西凤酒为典型代表。这种香型的白酒，以高粱为原料，采用续渣配料，土窖发酵等酿造工艺酿制而成。

The fifth is the phoenix-flavor Xifeng wine in Shaanxi Province. It's made from the long-brewed sorghum for a long time and then fermented in a mud pit.

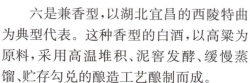

六是兼香型，以湖北宜昌的西陵特曲为典型代表。这种香型的白酒，以高粱为原料，采用高温堆积、泥窖发酵、缓慢蒸馏、贮存勾兑的酿造工艺酿制而成。

The sixth is mixed-flavor. Xiling Tequ is from Hubei Province. It is also made from sorghum，brewed at a very high temperature and then left in a mud pit for fermentation before slow distillation，and then being put into storage for blending.

任务 Tasks

单人活动 Individual Work

说说您自己国家有哪些名酒？并与老师和同学分享酒文化的不同。

Talk about the types of alcohol in your own country, and share the differences of drinking culture with your teachers and classmates.

第三节　传统茶文化

Unit Three　Traditional Tea Culture

中国茶文化是中国制茶、饮茶的文化,作为开门七件事(柴米油盐酱醋茶)之一,中国古人饮茶的历史已有数千年。茶文化不仅包含物质文化,更包含深厚的精神文明。唐代茶圣陆羽的《茶经》在历史上吹响了中华茶文化的号角。

按照制茶工艺可以分为绿茶、红茶、白茶、乌龙茶、砖茶和花茶六类。中国的茶具因历史阶段、地区、民族、饮茶习惯和方式的不同,所使用的材料、造型、工艺和称谓皆不相同。

Chinese Tea Culture is the culture of making and drinking tea. It is considered as one of the seven daily necessities (woods, rice, oil, salt, sauce, vinegar and tea). There is a thousand-year-history of drinking tea among Chinese ancestors. Chinese Tea Culture not only involves material culture but also profound spiritual culture. Lu Yu, the sage of tea from Tang Dynasty made a good extension of Chinese Tea Culture.

According to the tea production process, Chinese tea can be divided into six categories: green tea, black tea, white tea, oolong tea, brick tea and scented tea. Chinese tea sets vary according to the historical period, regions, ethnic groups, tea-drinking habits and ways. The material, modeling, craftwork and names used for tea sets are different as well.

 茶的起源 The Origin of Tea

据说,茶最早是在公元前 2737 年被中国的皇帝神农发现。这位皇帝喜欢将水烧开了喝,认为这样能起到净化作用,他的仆人也是这样做的。一天,在长途旅行中,皇帝和他的军队停下来休息。仆人为皇上烧水喝,碰巧一片野茶树的落叶飘到了水中,水便带上了一层褐

色。但没有人注意到,像往常一样,仆人将烧开了的水给皇上喝。皇帝喝后觉得精神气爽,从此就有了茶。

Tea is believed to have been discovered by the Chinese Emperor Shennong in 2737 B. C. It is said that the emperor liked drinking water boiled clean before he drank it, and that was what his servants usually did. One day, on a trip to a distant region, Shennong and his army stopped to have a rest. A servant began boiling water for him to drink, and a dry leaf from a wild tea bush fell into the water, tinging it brownish. But it was unnoticed and presented to the emperor anyway. The emperor drank it and found it very refreshing. Tea as a drink thus came into being.

虽然茶是什么时候作为可提神的药用草药并没有明确的历史记载,不过中国关于饮茶的记录被认为是最早的,可以追溯到公元前一千年。

While historically the origin of tea as a medicinal herb to keep drinkers awake is unclear, China is considered to have the earliest records of tea drinking, with documents dating back to the first millennium B.C.

 茶的分类 **Types of Tea**

在中国,通常按照生产加工方式将茶叶分为绿茶、红茶、白茶、乌龙茶、砖茶及花茶六个主要类别。加工茶叶的主要方式包括发酵、加热、干燥以及添加其他成分如花、草药、水果。

It is customary in China to classify many varieties of tea into six main categories：green tea, black tea, white tea, oolong tea, brick tea, and scented tea according to their production methods. They can be made by fermentation, heating, drying, and adding other ingredients like flowers, herbs, or fruits. These help to develop the special flavor of the raw tea leaves.

Green Tea

绿茶是中国所有茶叶中最受欢迎、产量最高的茶，绿茶是不经过发酵的，因其汤青茶绿故名为绿茶。著名的绿茶品种有杭州西湖龙井茶、江苏碧螺春茶、安徽黄山的毛峰茶和产于安徽六安县一带的六安瓜片茶。

Green tea is unfermented and the most popular tea. It's produced in the largest quantities in China. It is so named as the dried leaves and the infusion are both green shades. There are many famous green teas：Longjing from West Lake in Hangzhou,

Green Tea

Biluochun in Jiangsu, Maofeng from Yellow Mountain in Anhui and the Liu'an Guapian Tea produced from Liu'an County in Anhui.

Black Tea

红茶是经过发酵的茶，沏出的茶水颜色红艳。著名的红茶有安徽的祁红茶和云南的滇红茶。

Black tea is the fermented tea, and the color of its liquid is brilliant red. Qi black tea in Anhui Province and Dian black tea in Yunnan Province are famous black tea in China.

White Tea

白茶是一种表面满披白色茸毛的"轻微发酵茶",是中国茶类中的特殊珍品,白茶的表面覆盖了一层白色茸毛,故而得名。白茶为福建的特产,主要产区在福鼎、政和、松溪、建阳等地。冲泡出来的白茶为淡黄绿色,清澈而香气浓郁。著名的白茶品种为"白毫银针"和"白牡丹"。

The leaves of white tea are covered with white fuzz, hence its name. It is a local specialty of Fujian Province, mainly produced in Fuding, Zhenghe, Songxi and Jianyang counties. When steeped in boiling water, white tea bears a pale yellowish green. It is clear and fragrant. Baihao Yinzhen and White Peony are famous examples of white tea.

Oolong Tea

乌龙茶是一种半发酵的茶,既有绿茶的清香,又有红茶的浓郁。乌龙茶生长在悬崖上,采摘之难使乌龙茶成为了中国最珍贵的茶。最好的乌龙茶是产在福建武夷山的武夷岩茶。

Known as a half-fermented tea, oolong tea is an excellent combination of the freshness of green tea and the fragrance of black tea. Oolong tea grows on cliffs, making the picking process quite difficult. The best oolong tea is bohea, produced in the Wuyi Mountain of Fujian Province.

Brick Tea

砖茶就是被制成类似砖形状的茶,是将茶叶和茶杆放在一起压制成的薄板,是蒙古族、藏族等少数民族喜欢喝的茶。最有名的当属云南的普洱茶了。

Brick tea is made in the form of a brick. It is tea and

tea bar together compressed into a thin sheet. Mongolian，Tibetan and other ethnic minorities like drinking brick tea. The most famous is the Yunnan Pu'er tea.

Scented Tea

花茶是中国独有的一个茶类，是在茶叶中加入香花熏制而成的。可用的花有茉莉花、兰花、栀子花、玫瑰、桂花等，其中茉莉花用得最多。最有名的花茶是福建产的茉莉花茶。

Scented tea is specific to China，which is made by smoking tea leaves with fragrant flowers. The flowers available are jasmine，orchid，gardenia，rose and sweet-scented osmanthus. Jasmine，however，is the most popular of these. The most famous scented tea is jasmine tea from Fujian Province.

饮茶的习俗 Customs of Drinking Tea

中国饮茶历史最早，客来敬茶，以茶代酒，用茶示礼，历来是我国各民族的饮茶之道。"千里不同风，百里不同俗。"中国是一个多民族的国家，共有 56 个兄弟民族，由于所处地理环境和历史文化的不同，以及生活风俗的差异，使每个民族的饮茶风俗也各不相同。

Chinese tea drinking tradition is to serve tea to guests，offer it as a substitution for wine，and offering tea for presents are our country's etiquette. China is a multiethnic country including 56 ethnic groups. Due to various geographical conditions，history，culture and customs，each ethnicity's tea drinking custom is unique.

汉族饮茶大多推崇清饮，其方法就是将茶直接用滚开水冲泡，无须在茶汤中加入姜、椒、盐、糖之类佐料。最有汉族饮茶代表性的要数品龙井、啜乌龙、吃盖碗茶、泡九道茶和喝大碗茶了。

Han people require clear water when drinking tea. The

brewing method is to put the tea directly into boiling water without adding ingredients such as ginger，pepper，salt or sugar. The most common tea of the Han people are Longjing，oolong，Gaiwan tea and Jiudao tea.

藏族主要分布在中国西藏、云南、四川、青海等地区。藏族的酥油茶是以茶为主料，并加有多种食料经混合而成的液体饮料，喝起来咸里透香，甘中有甜，它既可暖身御寒，又能补充营养。偶尔，有客来访，可招待的东西很少，加上酥油茶的独特作用，因此，敬酥油茶便成了西藏人款待宾客的珍贵礼仪。

Zang ethnic group people are mainly distributed over Tibet，Yunnan，Sichuan，Qinghai and other regions. Tibetan tea uses buttered tea as the main ingredient，and adds a variety of food to mix into liquid beverages. It tastes salty，bitter and sweet. It makes people feel warm and get extra nutrition. Therefore，serving buttered tea to guests is an important part of their etiquette.

蒙古族主要居住在内蒙古及其边缘的一些省、区，喝咸奶茶是蒙古族人们的传统饮茶习俗。咸奶茶是将青砖茶或黑砖茶放入铁锅煮制而成。在牧区，他们习惯于"一日三餐茶"，却往往是"一日一顿饭"。通常一家人只在晚上放牧回家才正式用餐一次，但早、中、晚三次喝咸奶茶一般是不可缺少的。

The Mongolian ethnic minority mainly lives in Inner Mongolia and some other provinces and districts near by. Drinking salty milk tea is a traditional tea custom for Mongolian people. Salty milk tea is cooked by boiling the brick tea or black tea in a wok. In the pastoral areas，they say "tea at every meal，" but most people usually only eat an actual meal once a day. Usually the family only has one formal dinner in the evening after grazing. But drinking salty milk tea in the morning，afternoon and evening is an indispensable substitution for the other meals.

白族散居在我国西南地区，主要分布在风光秀丽的云南大理，这是一个好客的民族。在逢年过节、生辰寿诞、男婚女嫁、拜师学艺等喜庆日子里，或是在亲朋宾客来访之际，都会以"一苦、二甜、三回味"的三道茶款待。它告诫人们，凡事要多回味，切记先苦后甜的哲理。

The Bai ethnic group is scattered in southwest China and mainly distributed in the beautiful scenery of Dali in Yunnan Province. It's a hospitable region. Whenever people are on holidays，have a birthday，get married，go off for studies or pay their relatives or friends a visit，they usually serve them with a kind of tea whose taste is bitter，sweet and memorable. They also use this way to warn people that everything needs careful taste and there is no sweet without sweat.

四 中国的茶具 Chinese Tea Set

金属茶壶 Metal Teapot

中国茶具所用的不同材质有金属、瓷、陶、紫砂、漆、木头、竹子和玻璃。

Tea sets in China are made of various materials，including metal，porcelain，pottery，purple clay，lacquer，wood，bamboo and glass.

在唐代，金属茶具只有贵族才用得起，普通百姓通常用陶瓷茶具。宋朝，彩色釉茶具比较流行。到了元朝，瓷器茶具成为了主流。

Tea sets made of metal were reserved for the nobility，and civilians commonly used porcelain ware and earthen

青瓷茶壶 Celadon Teapot

白瓷茶壶 White Porcelain Teapot

紫砂茶壶 Ceramic Teapot

竹制茶壶 Bamboo Teapot

② 宜兴紫砂茶具曾是中国特有的手工制造陶土工艺品，已有 2 400 多年的历史。

Yixing purple-clay teapot was the specific hand-made pottery artware in China, and it has a history of more than 2,400 years.

ware in the Tang Dynasty. In the Song Dynasty, glazed tea sets of various colors were the fashion, while porcelain tea sets predominated in the Yuan Dynasty.

青瓷茶具因色泽青翠，用来冲泡绿茶，更有益汤色之美。白瓷茶具因色泽洁白，能反映出茶汤色泽，传热、保温性能适中，色彩缤纷，造型各异，堪称饮茶器合冲泡各类茶叶。

The Celadon tea set is often used to brew green tea because its green color can show the beauty of the tea. The white porcelain tea set can reflect the color of tea. It is considered as a treasure because it can transfer heat, and it have moderate thermal insulation properties, different colors and shapes. It is suitable for brewing all kinds of tea.

宜兴紫砂茶具②风格多样，造型多变，富含文化品位，具有三大特点，就是"泡茶不走味，贮茶不变色，盛暑不易馊"。

Yixing purple-clay teapot has both diverse styles and multiple appearances, which are rich in cultural taste. It has three characteristics, and they are the long-lasting fragrance of the tea made in it, luster in color of storing tea, fresh and pure in mid-summer.

四川的竹制茶具由内、外两部分组成，内层为陶瓷，其外围竹制，用来保护、完善内层。同时，有了外层的竹子，茶具拿起来也不会烫手。

Bamboo tea sets in Sichuan Province are made up of inner and outer bodies. The inner bodies are mostly porcelain and pottery tea sets, while the outer bamboo bodies are made to protect and delicate the inner frame. Moreover, the tea sets will be not too hot to touch with the overcoat.

在现代，玻璃器皿因其透明的质地和耀眼的光泽深受欢迎。用玻璃杯沏茶，还可以清楚地看到茶水真正的色泽和茶叶的柔和。但是，玻璃杯易碎，而且不隔热。

In modern times, glass utensils are warmly welcomed because of their transparent texture and dazzling luster. Making tea in a glass cup, you can clearly see the real color of the brew and the softness of the tea leaves. But glass tea cups break easily, and they are often too hot to touch.

任务 Tasks

1. 单人活动 Individual Work

说说您自己国家有哪些饮品？并与老师和同学分享不同的文化。

Talk about the drinks in your country, and share the differences of the culture with your teachers and classmates.

2. 小组活动 Group Work

搜索网站资料，查找中国的十大名茶，并填好下表。

Search for the information about the Top Ten famous Chinese tea and fill in the following form.

名称：Name：
产地：Place：
特点：Feature：

第三章　传统艺术
Chapter Three　Traditional Art

☞ 文化贴士11

　　中国是个历史悠久,幅员辽阔的国家。从远古时代开始,中国的世代祖辈们在这个广袤无垠的土地上繁衍、生存并孕育着中华璀璨的文明。作为世界四大文明古国之一,中国有着 5 000 多年的历史,其传统艺术等世界闻名。5 000 多年来,中国已经培养了许多伟大的思想家、发明家、政治家、战略家、文人和艺术家,创造着丰富的文化遗产和优秀的中国传统文化。本节主要从文化的角度去呈现传统艺术。

　　China is a large country with time-honored history. From the ancient times, the ancestors of Chinese labored, lived, and multiplied on this vast land, creating a splendid culture. As one of the four cradles of world's earliest civilizations, it has a recorded history of nearly 5,000 years. Throughout the history of Chinese civilization, its traditional culture has been renowned all over the world. During these 5,000 years, China has nurtured many great thinkers, inventors, statesmen, strategists, men of letters and artists, yielding a rich cultural heritage and fine cultural traditions. This chapter mainly presents Chinese traditional art from cultural aspects.

第一节　书法与绘画
Unit One　Calligraphy and Painting

一　书法 Calligraphy

中国传统书法、绘画、琴艺、棋艺构成了古代文人骚客（包括一些名门闺秀）修身养性所必须掌握的技能，故合称琴棋书画，即"文人四友"，展现着一个人的气质和文化素养。

Calligraphy and painting together with *Qin*（a general name for certain musical instrument）and *Qi*（Chinese Chess）make up the four skills for a learned and elegant scholar to pursue in ancient times. They were also considered as a good exercise to improve one's patience and concentration.

中国书法一般特指中文汉字的书写艺术。中国书法是以中国文化为内涵，以汉字为基础的独特视觉艺术。汉字是中国书法的组成部分，是中国文化的重要部分。中国书法包括篆书、楷书、草书、行书、隶书等。

Chinese calligraphy art refers to Chinese character writing in general. Chinese calligraphy is a cornerstone of Chinese culture, on the basis of Chinese unique visual art. Chinese characters are as much an important factor in Chinese calligraphy, as well as Chinese culture. Chinese calligraphy consists of five styles, including seal character, regular script, cursive hand, running hand and official script.

在中国博大精深的历史长河中,中国的书画艺术以其独特的艺术形式和艺术语言再现了这一历史性的嬗变过程。中国书画艺术在历史的嬗变中又以其互补性和独立性释读了汉族传统文化内涵。书、画创作所采用的工具与材料具有一致性。

Over the course of Chinese history, calligraphy has been constantly evolving to suit the needs of the language and the written word. Calligraphy and painting go hand-in-hand, complimenting each other as character mimics art and art mimics calligraphy. Thanks to the calligraphy, painting tools and materials are constantly being improved upon.

传统书法通过毛笔,将墨汁挥洒于纸上,形成独特优雅的毛笔笔画。

Traditional Chinese calligraphy uses brushes made from animal hair to apply ink to paper, producing uniquely graceful brushstrokes.

历经3 000多年的发展历程,书法已成为中国文化的代表性符号。

After 3,000 years of evolution, calligraphy has become a representative symbol of Chinese culture.

中国独有的文书工具,即文房四宝。安徽是文房四宝的故乡,湖笔、徽墨、宣纸、歙砚,文房四宝中三宝均源于安徽。笔、墨、纸、砚之名,起源于南北朝时期。

China has four special tools for writing，which they consider "treasures." Anhui Province is the home of four treasures of the study：writing brushes，*Huimo*，rice paper，and the inkstand. Pen，ink，paper and inkstone originated from the Northern and Southern Dynasties.

现代书写工具逐步取代毛笔，简体汉字也广为运用。但是，中国人将练习书法视为自我修养和个性表现的一种形式。将传统书法技艺运用于当代钢笔和圆珠笔，保留毛笔书法的形式和美观，形成新的书法形式"硬笔书法"。

Modern writing implements have gradually supplanted the brush，and simplified Chinese characters have reformed traditional complex forms. But Chinese people still practice calligraphy as a means of self-cultivation and self-expression. Traditional calligraphic techniques have been applied to writing with fountain pens and ballpoint pens，preserving the form and beauty of brush writing in a new style known as "hard calligraphy."

中国书法是汉字的书写艺术，中国的汉字具有天然的美感，无论字体如何变化，都体现了中华民族对客观世界的抽象概括，对生命的深层次思考。

Chinese calligraphy is the art of writing Chinese characters. Chinese characters have a natural aesthetic feeling，no matter the font，and reflect the Chinese abstract impression of the objective world and the deeper meaning of life.

二 中国画 Chinese Painting

国画一词起源于汉代,汉朝人认为中国是居天地之中者,所以称为中国,将中国的绘画称为"中国画",简称"国画"。

The term, Traditional Chinese painting, originated in the Han Dynasty. Han Dynasty people thought that China was in the heavens and on the earth, so they called it China. Thus paintings were called "the traditional Chinese painting."

女史箴图 Palace Lady, attributed to Gu Kaizhi(317—407)from 4‑5th Century Tang copy.

传统中国画运用毛笔,沾上墨汁与颜料在轻薄丝绸或宣纸上作画,最后装裱成轴。中国画注重线条的连贯性和表现力,认为表意重于画形。

Traditional Chinese painting uses brushes to apply ink and pigment to thin silk or paper, which is then mounted on scrolls. Great importance is placed on fluidity and expressiveness of the line. In Chinese painting, revealing essence is more important than representing form.

早期的绘画以宗教题材为主。公元7世纪后,因社会追求个体与自然的和谐,受这一理念的影响,新的画派诞生,提倡打破有形想象力的局限,运用象征手法表达内心世界。至此,绘画的主题渐渐由宗教人物转为自然风光,形成山水画和花鸟画两大流派。

Early Chinese painting was primarily religiously oriented. But after the 7th century A. D. , Chinese painting was influenced by the holistic concept of seeking harmony between Humanity and Nature. A new school of painting arose that advocated breaking the bonds of concrete imagery and using symbolism to represent the inner world. As a result，subject matter gradually changed from religious figures to natural scenery，including landscape and "bird and flower" paintings.

国画以其原始的风格和独特的民族特色而闻名于世。在过去的几个世纪里，无数艺术家追求艺术的实践使其种类繁多。

Traditional Chinese Painting is famous for its original style and distinctive representations of the world. Over the centuries，the practice of countless artists evolved into an art subdivided into a multitude of schools with some traits in common.

在绘画表达方式上，中国传统绘画主要分为写意，即"绘画的感觉"，以夸张的形式和自由使用墨水著称；另一种叫工笔，即意义细致的笔法，以严格和详细表达著称。

In terms of the mode of expression，traditional Chinese painting mainly falls into two schools. The Xieyi School, literally "painting the feeling," marked by exaggeration of form and liberal use of ink; the other school called *Gongbi*，meaning meticulous brushwork，characterized by strict and detailed representation of the subject.

清朝成就最为突出是郑燮，著名的扬州画家（1693—1765年），又名郑板桥，江苏兴化人，清代杰出画家。一生主要客居扬州，以卖画为生。"扬州八怪"之一，擅画兰、竹、石、松、菊等植物，其中画竹五十余年。

Zheng Xie, a famous painter of Yangzhou（1693—1765），was a prominent painter in the Qing Dynasty. He spent most of his life in Yangzhou，selling paintings for a living. He was good at painting orchids，bamboos，chrysanthemums，stones，pines and other plants. He painted bamboo for more than 50 years.

第二节　雕刻与雕塑
Unit Two　Carving and Sculpture

 雕刻 Carving

　　"雕刻是一切艺术的鼻祖"这句话真实表述了中国的雕刻艺术。中国雕刻艺术伴随着中华文明的发展繁荣。中国雕刻分玻璃雕、核雕、玉雕、木雕、石雕、竹刻以及造像和其他雕刻门类。

　　"Carving is the forerunner of all art." This saying truly describes the Chinese carving arts. Chinese carvings consist of glass carving, fruit core carving, jade carving, wood carving, bamboo

carving, brick carving, statues and other kinds of carving.

　　玻璃雕是将两种色料深浅各异的玻璃经高温融合,采用雕花技术,并剔除多余部分,精雕细磨而成的手工艺品至今已有300多年的历史。

Glass carving is a kind of art. Two different colors of glass are mixed together under a high temperature. Then the artist carves the beautiful patterns and grinds it to a smooth finish. This skill has endured since it's innovation over 300 years ago.

　　核雕是在核桃、橄榄核、杏核等果核上,雕刻出各种人物,走兽、山水、楼、台、亭、阁等图像的一种冥界微型雕刻工艺。核雕的工序繁复,

主要工具为锉、凿、钻等。受果核本身的局限，一般采用立雕、浮雕等工艺。雕刻时要充分利用果核的形状，麻纹、质地，因材施艺，精心布局。核雕在公元14世纪已达到了很高的水平。

The materials of sculpture are all kinds of fruit cores. The master can carve the pattern of man，animal，landscape，pavilion and building on a very small core. The procedures of this are very complex. The main tools include filling, chiseling and drilling，etc. Due to the limitation of the shape of the material，we can only use solid or embossment art style. The artist must also make full use of the shape and texture. The skill of core sculpture has been improving since the 14th century.

玉雕，即在玉石上雕刻形象的工艺。它是一种古老的工艺品，已有八千多年的悠久历史。中国是世界上主要产玉国，蕴藏丰富。中国玉雕工艺源远流长，技法成熟，工序繁复，玉色泽纯净，质地坚硬，中国古人常用玉来比喻美好事物。

Just as its name suggests, jade sculpture is using jade to create a piece of art. It also has a long history of more than 8,000 years. China is abundant in jade. The skill of jade sculpture has been well developed in China over a long time. It has a well-designed process and skill. The purity and hardness of the jade are often used to symbolize the beautiful things in ancient China.

木雕，是以各种木材及木根为材料进行雕刻的工艺，是传统雕刻工艺中的重要门类。木雕一般选用质地细密坚韧，不易变形的树种作为材料雕刻而成。中国木雕种类繁多，遍布大江南北。在木雕艺术中，工艺木雕是

雕刻艺术中的精华，一般是由经验丰富、技艺精湛的老艺人或工艺美术设计、雕刻，再由工艺娴熟的工人大量雕刻复制。而艺术木雕一般是由作者一手设计制作而成的独件作品。

Wood sculpture is the art of carving wood，such as tree roots or trunks. It is the main stream of the traditional sculpture arts. The type of wood is usually the one that is hardest and has the least knots or other incongruities. The types of wood sculptures are diverse and widespread. And craft-wood sculpture is an elite form of sculpture. The best works are carved by experienced masters，then apprentices will copy again and again. Wood sculpture requires the masters to put the finishing touches on all the works by themselves.

石雕就是以各类石料为原材料制成的民间工艺品。中国石雕艺术有悠久的历史，至今仍保留有 7,000 多年前的石雕作品。中国石材资源丰富，石雕种类繁多，色泽纹理绚丽多彩。小型石雕多选用青田石、寿山石等颜色丰富的石料。石雕艺人用雕刀、凿子、车钻、刺条等工具，经过设计、打抷、雕刻、配垫、上蜡等工序把一块石头变成精美的工艺品。

Stone carving is an art of using stone as the material. The earliest work we have is over 7,000 years old. China is abundant in stone resources，which makes stone carving a diverse and proliferant. The process of stone carving includes designing，carving，tray-making and wax-making，which can help to make a rough stone into a beautiful art crafts.

竹雕，是在竹制的器物上雕刻多种装饰图案和文字，或用竹根雕刻成各种陈设摆件。中国是世界上最早使用竹制品的国家，竹雕工艺

历史悠久，远古的精兵巧器，公元前 8 世纪的简书，都是竹雕的前身。公元 5 世纪，竹雕逐渐成为一种艺术。公元 14 世纪，竹雕大盛，竹雕工艺发展到空前的鼎盛阶段，在历史上留下了辉煌的一页。

Bamboo can be used as the material of carving. The words or drawings are carved on the bamboo using utensils and roots. The bamboo utensils were first used in China. Bamboo weapons and books from the 8th century B. C. are the source of the bamboo carving. By the 5th century A. D. , bamboo carving had become a standard art form. It flourished in the 14th century A. D. and made its mark on history.

二 雕塑 Sculpture

　　最初的雕塑可以从原始社会的石器和陶器算起，这是中国雕塑的序幕。造型多样的陶器，为中国雕塑的多向性发展奠定了基础。

Original sculptures from primitive societies were made using stone and pottery. These would provide platforms with which later Chinese civilizations would model their sculpture upon, diversifying and improving upon primitive methods.

　　在中国浙江出土的陶塑作品，距今已有 7 000 年的历史。中国古代雕塑题材主要是陵墓雕塑、宗教雕塑和劳动生活及名俗雕塑。陶文化中以秦兵马俑和唐三彩最为著目。

Some of the pottery found in Zhejiang Province were produced as much as 7,000 years ago. Its subjects were mainly focused on the mausoleum, religions, daily life and folk-custom. Later in history, Terracotta Warriors and *Tang Sancai* ceramics would become the most famous in the pottery culture.

　　散落于中国各石窟和佛寺中的宗教雕塑是中国传统雕刻的缩影。

云冈石窟和龙门石窟中巨大宏伟的佛像向全世界展示了中国无与伦比的雕刻传统。通常这些佛像均雕饰精美服饰,巧妙地表现出佛像的外形和气韵。

The Buddhist statues found in China's grottoes and temples represent the epitome of traditional Chinese sculpture. The massive and majestic Buddhas of the Yungang and Longmen Grottoes have brought China's extraordinary sculptural tradition to the eyes of the world. These sculptures often feature beautifully carved clothing. They skillfully portray the form and dynamism of their subjects.

秦始皇兵马俑在 1974 年出土,这一地下军队中有各类士兵,两两相异,面部形态真实,表情各异。陶俑的制作必定有大量工匠的参与,才能展现出如此多样的技艺。

The great underground terracotta army of Emperor Qin Shihuang was first unearthed in 1974. The army includes a wide variety of soldiers, no two alike, all with highly realistic carved faces and unique expressions. These figures must have been created by a large number of craftsmen in order to display such diverse techniques.

俑是中国古代坟墓中陪葬用的偶人。俑的质料以木、陶质最常见。俑的形象,主要有奴仆、舞乐、士兵,并常附有鞍马、牛车等。

Figurines in Chinese ancient grave tombs are burial dolls. The materials of the figurines are commonly wood and pottery. Tomb figures depict slaves, dancing girls, soldiers, horses, oxen, etc.

陶马与真马一般大小，一匹匹形体健壮，肌肉丰满。那跃跃欲试的样子，好像一声令下，就会撒开四蹄，腾空而起，踏上征程。

Taoma is a life-size horse figurine. Just looking at it causes the viewer to have the wish to try to command it, demanding it take off on a journey.

唐三彩，汉族古代陶瓷烧制工艺的珍品，全名唐代三彩釉陶器，是盛行于唐代的一种低温釉陶器，釉彩有黄、绿、白、褐、蓝、黑等色，而以黄、绿、白三色为主，所以人们习惯称之为"唐三彩"。因唐三彩最早、最多出土于洛阳，亦有"洛阳唐三彩"之称。

The Tang Sancai is a kind of treasure from the ancient Han ceramics. The full name is the Three Colored Glaze Pottery. It is a low-temperature glazed pottery, glazed with yellow，green，white，brown，blue，black and other colors，but mainly based on yellow，green and white. People used to call it "tang" because it was most prevalent in the Tang Dynasty. The earliest discovery was unearthed in Luoyang, so most also have the name of "Luoyang Tang."

任务　Tasks

单人活动　Individual Work

你知道下面这些雕刻作品出自哪些著名旅游景点吗？

Do you know which tourist attractions the following pictures are taken from?

（　　）　　　　　　　　　　　（　　）

（　　）　　　　　　　　　　　（　　）

A. 秦始皇兵马俑　　　　　Terracotta Warriors of Emperor Qin Shihuang

B. 云冈石窟　　　　　　　the Yungang Grottoes

C. 龙门石窟　　　　　　　the Longmen Grottoes

D. 莫高窟　　　　　　　　the Mogao Grottoes

第三节　音乐和戏剧
Unit Three　Music and Drama

一　音乐 Music

纵观中国历史,音乐存在的形式多种多样。最初的中式音乐主要为舞蹈进行器乐伴奏,汉代以后,声乐和舞蹈的新形式逐渐盛行。

Music has existed in different forms throughout Chinese history. The earliest Chinese music was primarily instrumental accompanied by dance. After the Han Dynasty（202 B.C.—A.D. 220）, a new form of vocal music and dance became popular.

音乐的历史与**乐器**①的发展史密不可分。与西方乐器类似,传统中式乐器也是种类繁多,其中拉弦乐器有二胡、板胡,弹拨乐器有琵琶和筝,吹奏乐器有笛和唢呐,打击乐器有鼓和锣。

The history of music and the development of musical instruments are inseparable. Traditional Chinese instruments, like those of the West, encompass many types. They include bowed string instruments, such as the *Erhu* and *Banhu*; plucked string instruments, such as the *Pipa* and *Zheng*; wind instruments, such as the Flute and *Suona*; percussion instruments, such as the drum and

① 早在新石器时代,中国的先人们就发明了骨笛和埙——一种陶制管乐器。1978 年出土了一组编钟,其历史可以追溯至战国时期。

As early as the Neolithic Age, the ancestors of Chinese invented the bone flute and the *xun*, a wind pottery instrument. A set of bells dating from the Warring States Period （475—221 B.C.）was unearthed in 1978.

② 二胡有中国小提琴的美誉，是胡琴家族中受欢迎的器乐。

The *Erhu* is called the Chinese Violin or the Chinese two-string fiddle. It was a popular instrument in the Huqin family.

gong *luo*.

二胡② 始于唐朝，已有一千多年的历史，二胡器乐源自古蒙古。它最早起源于我国古代北部地区的一个少数民族，那时叫"奚琴"。奚琴起源于中亚地区，于公元 10 世纪传入中国。

The *Erhu* can be traced back to proto-Mongolic instruments introduced to China more than a thousand years ago. It is believed to have evolved from the Xiqin. The Xiqin is believed to originate from the Xi people of Central Asia, and came to China in the 10th century.

华彦钧，又名阿炳，是江苏无锡的一位民间盲艺人，是闻名中外的杰出的民间音乐家，由于他的艺术深受人们的欢迎，当地人民亲切地叫他"瞎子阿炳"。二胡名曲有《二泉映月》。

Hua Yanjun（A Bing，1893—1950）was a blind street musician in Wuxi. Shortly before his death in 1950, he recorded several famous songs，the best-known being "Moon Reflected on Second Spring."

《茉莉花》是中国民歌，在中国及世界广为传颂，被誉为"中国的第二国歌"。该首歌曲展现了少女热爱生活，爱花、惜花、怜花，想采花又不敢采的羞涩心情。

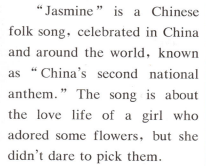

"Jasmine" is a Chinese folk song, celebrated in China and around the world, known as "China's second national anthem." The song is about the love life of a girl who adored some flowers, but she didn't dare to pick them.

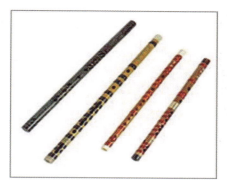

笛子是中国广为流传的吹奏乐器，因为是用天然竹材制成，所以也称为"竹笛"。笛子的表现力非常丰富，它既能演奏悠长高亢的旋律，又能表现辽阔、宽广的情调。

The flute is a widely circulated musical instrument in China because it is made from natural bamboo, so it's also known as the "bamboo flute." The expressive force of the flute is very rich, and it can play a long and loud melody, and will show a vast and broad tone.

笛子的表现力不仅仅在于优美的旋律，它还能表现大自然的各种声音，比如模仿各种鸟叫等。

The expressive feeling of the flute is not just about beautiful melody. It can also show the sounds of nature, such as imitating all kinds of birds.

弹拨乐器的历史悠久，种类形制繁多，是极富特色的一类弦乐器。琵琶已经有两千多年的历史，是骑在马上弹奏的乐器。最早被称为"琵琶"的乐器大约在中国秦朝出现。

Walking Around Jiangsu

Plucked instruments have a long history. There are various kinds of shapes and highly characteristic string instruments. The *Pipa* has a history of more than 2,000 years. The earliest known *Pipa* instrument appeared in China during the Qin Dynasty.

二 戏剧 Drama

中国的民间艺术种类繁多,昆曲和京剧是最具代表性的。

The Chinese drama includes both traditional opera and modern theater. There are many other Chinese folk arts. The Kunqu Opera and Peking Opera are the most typical.

地域差异和各地方言孕育了大量的地方戏曲,著名的**昆曲**③就是源于长江三角洲地区。因其曲词典雅、行腔婉转、表演细腻,故历史、文化、艺术价值极高,2001 年,联合国教科文组织宣布为第一批"人类口头和非物质遗产代表作"。

Differences in location and dialect gave rise to many regional forms of traditional Chinese opera. Kunqu Opera originated in the Yangtze River Delta region. With its beautiful arias, elegant lyrics and subtle acting, Kunqu Opera has a great historical, cultural and artistic value. In 2001, Kunqu Opera was designated by UNESCO as a masterpiece of the Oral and Intangible Heritage of Humanity.

昆曲是中国最古老的歌剧形式之一,被认为是许多其他类型的传统戏剧之源。它起源于江苏省昆山地区,是比较流行的昆山地方戏,在明朝和清朝达到顶峰。它被誉为"中国戏曲的活化石",中国传统文化艺术的代表。

Kunqu Opera is one of the oldest operatic forms in China and is considered the mother of many other types of traditional operas. It originated from early folk opera popular in Kunshan, Jiangsu Province and reached its peak of popularity by the late Ming Dynasty and early Qing Dynasty. It is called a living fossil of Chinese Opera and is representative of Chinese traditional cultural art.

昆曲的腔调是其一大特色,一唱三叹,"以字行腔",体现了昆曲的

③ 昆曲《牡丹亭》,中国戏剧史上的巅峰之作,是最能体现昆曲精致浪漫的经典剧目。
Kunqu Opera *The Peony Pavilion* is the best known work in Chinese dramatic history and is the play that can bring the delicacy and romance of Kunqu Opera into full play.

畅游江苏

阴柔之美。昆剧的表演拥有一整套"载歌载舞"的严谨表演形式。

The tone of Kunqu Opera is one of the characteristics，containing "expression with clear articulation，" embodying the feminine beauty of Kunqu Opera. Kunqu Opera performance also has a unique style. It has a strong，exquisite and lyric movement，accompanied by harmonic singing and dancing.

京剧是中国"国粹"，它的行当全面、表演成熟、气势宏美，是近代**中国传统戏曲**④的代表。出现于18—19世纪，因其地域分布最广，观众人数最多，被认为是中国文化的精髓。京剧根据舞台角色划分为生、旦、净、丑四种类型，京剧表演的四种艺术手法：唱、念、做、打，也是京剧表演四项基本功。

Peking Opera or Beijing Opera is a form of traditional Chinese theatre which combines music，vocal performance，mime，dance and acrobatics. It arose in the late 18th century and became fully developed and recognized by the mid-19th century. It consists of the Male Role（Sheng），the Female Role（Dan），the Painted Face Male（Jing），and the Comedy Actor or Clown（Chou）. Peking Opera performers utilize four main skills：sing，speech，dance-acting and combat.

④ 中国传统戏曲被认为是世界上三大古代的歌剧之一，与希腊悲剧和喜剧、印度梵文歌剧齐名。

Chinese traditional opera is considered one of the world's three ancient operas, together with Greek tragedy and comedy, and Indian Sanskrit opera.

京剧已有 200 多年的历史，是中国的国剧。与其他地方戏相比，京剧享有更高的声誉，但其实京剧融合了多种地方戏的元素。

Peking Opera has a history of more than 200 years and is China's national opera. Compared with other local operas, Peking Opera enjoys a higher reputation，but in fact Peking Opera is a blend of various elements of local operas.

京剧是 1840 年以后正式形成的，慈禧太后（1835—1908年）是一个京剧爱好者，在位期间京剧发展得更快。经典京剧剧目和第一代大师的名字，经过人民的传诵，并最终在全国各地普遍存在。

It was after 1840 that Peking Opera formally took shape, growing even faster during the reign of the Empress Dowager Cixi (1835—1908)，who was an opera enthusiast. Classic Peking Opera repertoires and the names of the first-generation masters were on the lips of the people in Beijing，and eventually became prevalent around the country.

梅兰芳（1894—1961）是最著名的京剧表演艺术家。20 世纪 30 年代梅兰芳在美国演出并获得加州大学和波莫纳大学的荣誉学位。他是京剧海外演出的第一人，将京剧介绍给全世界的观众。

Mei Lanfang(1894—1961) is one of the most famous artists of Peking Opera. Mei Lanfang performed across the United States in

1930s, receiving honorary degrees from the University of California and Pomona College. He was the first Chinese artist to perform traditional Chinese opera abroad and to introduce it to an international audience.

京剧演员的脸谱和戏服都很精美，但布景十分简单。

Peking Opera actors' make-up and costumes are very beautiful，yet by contrast the set is very simple.

任务   Tasks

小组活动   Group Work

看图，将列表中的信息与图片连起来。

Look at the pictures and match the information in each table.

( ) ( ) ( )

( ) ( ) ( )

( ) ( ) ( )

A. 老生（Lao Sheng，a middle-aged or old man）

B. 小生（Xiao Sheng，young man）

C. 武生（Wu Sheng，acrobat）

D. 老旦（Lao Dan，old woman）

E. 武旦（Wu Dan，female acrobat）

F. 青衣（Qing Yi，noble woman of good quality and character）

G. 刀马旦（Dao Ma Dan，warrior woman）

H. 净（Jing，high-ranking army generals or bandits，warriors or officials）

I. 丑（Chou，clown）

2. 小组活动 Group Work

为左图的乐器找到对应的演奏名曲并课后欣赏。

Match the musical instruments with the related ancient famous music，and try to appreciate them after class.

Mighty Mountain and Flowing River（Gao Shan Liu Shui，高山流水）

Guang Ling Verse（Guang Ling Verse 广陵散）

Wild Geese（Ping Sha Luo Yan 平沙落雁）

Besieged（Shi Mian Mai Fu 十面埋伏）

Mei Flower（Mei Hua San Nong 梅花三弄）

Sunset（Xi Yang Xiao Gu 夕阳箫鼓）

3. 单人活动 Individual Work

请介绍一个你家乡的民间艺术。

Please introduce one of the folk arts in your hometown.

第四章　传统手工艺

Chapter Four　Traditional Handicrafts

👆 文化贴士12

　　手工艺是中国传统文化的重要组成部分,是指以手工劳动进行制作的具有独特艺术风格的工艺美术。本质上讲,手工艺是一种创意打扮人们生活的文化,是一种满足人的物质及精神生活需要的造物艺术。手工艺品指的是纯手工或借助工具制作的产品,蕴涵着人类文明之始的工艺文化,能够传达文化内涵,并富有装饰性、功能性和传统性。

　　随着人类现代生活方式的改变,许多传统手工艺开始衰落。20世纪后期以来,保护和发展民族民间文化已成为各国文化发展的重要课题。

Handicraft is an important part of Chinese traditional culture. It refers to an art and craft of handmade processes and unique artistic styles. In essence, handicraft is a kind of culture decorating people's lives creatively and a special form of artistic creation to meet people's material and spiritual needs. Handicrafts are made completely by hand or by using only simple tools. From the beginning of human civilization, people have been practicing and creating handicrafts for decorative, functional and traditional purposes to convey the cultural connotations.

With the transformation of human lifestyle in modern society, many of the traditional crafts declined. Therefore the protection and development of national folk culture has become an important subject for each country since the late 20th century.

　　中国传统手工艺是中华艺术的重要组成部分,既体现了工艺美术的一般特征,又显示了中华文化的鲜明个性。中国工匠们利用不同材质的原料创造出丰富多彩、巧夺天工的各类手工艺品,充分展现了中国人的卓越创造力和丰富生活情趣。

Traditional handicraft is an important part of Chinese arts. It not only embodies the general features of arts and crafts but also suggests the distinctive characteristics of Chinese culture. Making use of different raw materials, Chinese artists have produced diversified and exquisite handiwork which fully exhibits the excellent creativity and interests of the Chinese.

江苏是我国古代文明的发祥地之一,文化遗产资源十分丰厚,不仅有大量的物质文化遗产,也有丰富的非物质文化遗产。悠久的历史、发达的经济、灿烂的文化、优越的自然条件,孕育了丰富多彩、形式各样的传统手工艺。

江苏传统手工艺品类型多样,有丝织品、刺绣、陶瓷、剪纸、灯彩、金陵金箔、漆器、玉器、雕版印刷、苏扇、花边、扎染、蓝印花布、风筝、泥人、木版年画、微雕、贝雕、桃雕、根雕、叶雕、梳篦、留青竹刻等。这些手工艺品技艺精湛、承载着丰富的文化底蕴,既有传承,又有创新,并具有极高的艺术价值和实用价值,在国内外都享有很高的声誉。

Jiangsu is one of the birthplaces of ancient Chinese civilization, with a very rich cultural heritage. It has not only the massive material heritage, but also abundant non-material cultural heritage. Glorious history, a well-developed economy, splendid culture and advantageous natural conditions fostered traditional handicraft with rich diversity and various forms.

Various types of Jiangsu traditional handicrafts include silk fabric, embroidery, ceramic, paper-cutting, lantern-making, Jinling gold foil, lacquerware, jade ware, block printing, Suzhou fan, lace, tie-dye, blue calico, kite, clay figurine, woodblock print, miniature, shell carving, peach pit carving, root carving, leaf carving, comb-making, Liuqing bamboo carving and so on. These handicrafts are of exquisite craftsmanship, carry a wealth of cultural connotation, contain both tradition and innovation, possess high artistic value and practical value, and enjoy high reputations both at home and aboard.

 一　丝织 Silk Weaving

丝是中国对世界的贡献之一。中国是世界最早养蚕织绸的国家。传说**黄帝**[①]的妻子嫘祖教会了中国古代人民缫丝技术。

Silk is one of China's greatest contributions to the world. China was the first country to manufacture and use silk. According

① 黄帝是华夏民族始祖,人文初祖,中国远古时期部落联盟首领。

The Yellow Emperor is the primogenitor of the Chinese nation, the initiator of Chinese civilization and the Chinese ancient tribal leader.

to the legend, Lai Zu, wife of the Yellow Emperor, taught the ancient Chinese people the technique of sericulture.

自古以来,丝绸一直是中国出口商品之一。公元前 2 世纪(西汉时期),中国精美的丝绸已开始出口,其中一部分被运送到韩国和日本,但是大多数被带在骆驼背上,沿着著名的"丝绸之路"到达中东,最终到达西欧。丝绸是中国古老文化的象征,对促进世界人类文明的发展作出了不可磨灭的贡献。

Since ancient times, silk has been one of China's primary exports. Chinese fine silks were exported during the Western Han Dynasty in the second century B. C. A portion of the exports were shipped to Korea and Japan, but the majority was carried on camels' back along the famous caravan route known as the "Silk Road" to the Middle East, and eventually reaching Western Europe. As a symbol of ancient culture, Chinese silk made an indelible contribution to promote the development of the world civilization.

丝织品种繁多,其中云锦、宋锦、缂丝和苏绣因其丰富的文化内涵和工艺最为著名。

Silk fabrics come in a wide variety, among which Yunjin brocade, Song brocade, *Kesi* and Su embroidery are best known for their rich culture and techniques.

云锦是中国传统的提花丝制工艺品,是我国优秀传统文化的杰出代表,至今已有一千六百年历史。公元 417 年在建康(今南京)设立专门管理织锦的官署——锦蜀,被看作是南京云锦正式诞生的标志。

"Yunjin" is a general term for the traditional jacquard silk

fabric. As the most prominent representation of our nation's traditional culture，it has a history of 1,600 years. The building of the officially-run weaving factory "Jin Bureau" in Jiankang（present Nanjing）is viewed as the birth of Nanjing Yunjin Brocade in A.D. 417.

作为**中国四大名锦**②之首，云锦过去是专供皇族享用或作为贵赐织物，如今云锦还保持着传统的特色和独特的技艺。南京云锦因其色泽光丽灿烂，美如天上云霞而得名，其用料考究，织造精细，图案精美。

As top one of China's four famous brocades，Nanjing Yunjin Brocade was used exclusively by the imperial houses and as gifts bestowed by the emperors to princes or senior officials. Today，it is still woven by hand with traditional characteristics and unique techniques. Yunjin Brocades are famous for their exquisite technology，elegant patterns and smooth texture. The patterns are various and as beautiful as the clouds in the sky，hence it was named "Yunjin."

2009 年，南京云锦成功入选联合国《人类非物质文化遗产代表作名录》。

In 2009，Nanjing Yunjin Brocade was selected as a candidate for the Human Intangible Culture Heritage list of masterpiece at UNESCO.

② 中国四大名锦包括南京云锦、四川成都蜀锦、江苏苏州宋锦和广西壮锦。

Chinese Four Famous Brocades include Nanjing Brocade，Chengdu Brocade，Suzhou Brocade and Zhuang Brocade.

思考 Question

请你说一说陶器和瓷器有什么不同？

What are the differences between porcelain and pottery?

二 陶瓷 Ceramics

陶瓷的发展史是中华文明史的一个重要组成部分。在中国，制陶技艺的产生可追溯到新石器时代。制陶普遍存在于世界诸多古老文明中。但中国新石器时期的陶器特别是彩陶，从数量到质量，都为其他地区所不及。

The development history of ceramics is an important part of China's civilization. In China, ceramic production goes back to the Neolithic Age. Pottery making was widespread among many ancient civilizations in the world. However, China's pottery, especially painted pottery, during the Neolithic Age, was unrivaled both in quantity and quality.

③ "唐三彩"：因常用黄、绿、褐等色釉装饰而有斑斓变化，故名"三彩"。

Sancai is a type of ceramics using three colors, usually yellow, green and brown to color it for decoration.

④ 五大名窑指的是钧窑、汝窑、官窑、哥窑、定窑。

Five Famous Kilns include *Jun*, *Ru*, *Guan*, *Ge* and *Ding* Kiln.

魏晋南北朝时期，中国进入瓷器时代。唐代的"**唐三彩**"③鲜明而典型地反映了唐代雍容博大、清新华灿的时代面貌。宋代，中国传统瓷艺达到最高美学境界。**五大名窑**④所取得的卓越成就，使中国在人类制瓷史上登峰造极。元代统治者崇尚白瓷。白瓷的突飞猛进促成了元明清三代彩绘青花瓷的猛然崛起。

China entered a porcelain era during the Wei, Jin, the Southern and Northern Dynasties. *Sancai* typically reflects the elegance, resplendence and magnificence of the Tang Dynasty.

The Song Dynasty saw the aesthetic peak of traditional Chinese ceramics. The exceptional achievements made by the five famous kilns at the time led China to be the center of ceramic manufacturing. The rulers of the Yuan Dynasty held white porcelain in high esteem，which led to the rapid development of white porcelain，after which blue-and-white ware decorated with colored paintings sprung rapidly.

景德镇因其悠久的制瓷历史而被誉为"瓷都"。

Jingdezhen is renowned for its long history of porcelain production and has been acclaimed as the "Porcelain Capital of China."

宜兴，位于江苏省太湖西岸，是中国著名的陶都和世界制壶中心。宜兴制陶史可追溯到新石器时代。宜兴生产的陶器有 6 500 种之多，其中以紫砂器最为著名。

Located on the western shore of Taihu Lake in Jiangsu Province，Yixing is the pottery capital of China and the world center of teapot making. The history of ceramic production can be traced back to the Neolithic Age. Yixing is best known for its purple clay ware，though it produces 6,500 varieties of products.

紫砂是一种介于陶器和瓷器之间的陶瓷制品，结构致密，质地古朴自然。紫砂器无论是什么本色，在其表面皆隐含着若有似无的紫光，使其具有质朴高雅的质感，故称为"紫砂"。

Purple-clay pottery is a pottery product that is somewhere between pottery and porcelain. It is set apart by its dense

structure, simple and natural texture. The purple-clay products made of this kind of clay all reflect purple light on the surface, no matter what color lacquer has been applied. This endows it with natural and refined texture, so it is called "purple-clay pottery."

紫砂陶按功能主要有茶壶、花瓶、罐子等,其中又以紫砂壶最为有名。紫砂壶是集诗词、绘画、雕刻及手工制造于一体的工艺品。紫砂壶经久耐用,高温不易裂,用紫砂壶泡茶不变味,存茶不变色,时间越久,茶越醇厚。

According to their functions, the purple-clay products can be classified into teapots, flowerpots, jars, etc. among which the purple-clay teapot is the most famous. It combines poetry, painting, carving and handicraft into one. Meanwhile, it is durable and not likely to crack even in high temperatures. Tea made in a purple-clay teapot can retain its fragrance for a unusually long time without going stale.

三 剪纸 Paper-Cutting

剪纸是一种用剪刀或刻刀在纸上剪刻花纹,并将其粘贴在墙壁、窗户、门楣和天花板上的手工艺品。剪纸起源于中国,有着悠久的历史,深受普通大众欢迎。剪纸最早出现于**南北朝时期**⑤(公元 420—581)。

Paper-cutting refers to handicrafts made by cutting paper with scissors to form different patterns and pasting them on walls, windows, doors and

⑤ 南北朝时期(公元 420—581)是中国历史上的一段大分裂时期,也是历史上非常重要的时期,上承秦汉文明,下启隋唐盛世。

The Northern and Southern Dynasties(A. D. 420—581) was a complicated time, though it was also an important period in Chinese history that connects the Qin-Han civilization and the Sui-Tang civilization.

ceilings. With their long history, paper cutting, which originated in China, has been very popular among the local ordinary people. The first paper-cutting can be traced back to the Northern and Southern Dynasties（A. D. 420—581）.

作为中国最流行的民间艺术之一，剪纸最初来源于向祖先祭祀的宗教仪式或者作为刺绣的纸样。一千年前，剪纸开始用于装饰。据史书记载，唐代的女人用剪纸来做头饰。在宋朝的时候剪纸成为礼品的包装。

As one of the most popular folk arts, it's said that it originated from religious ceremonial offerings or sacrifices. A thousand years ago, paper-cutting was used for decoration. According to historical books, women in the Tang Dynasty used paper-cutting as head dresses. In the Song Dynasty, it was repurposed for the decoration of gifts.

剪纸是一种视觉上非常独特的中国手工艺品，全凭手工完成的精确的线条和独特的图案使得它能够独树一帜。经过千百年的发展，现在剪纸已经成为民间艺术一种非常普遍的装饰方式。

Paper-cutting is a very distinctive visual art of Chinese handicrafts. It still stands out for its charm—the exact lines and

ingenious patterns which are all hand-made. After hundreds of years' development, now it has become a very popular means of decoration among folk arts.

扬州剪纸的历史可追溯到2 000年前的隋代,使扬州成为剪纸最早流行的地区之一。

Yangzhou paper-cutting, with a history of 2,000 years, dates back to the Sui Dynasty, making Yangzhou one of the places where paper-cutting first became popular.

隋代,扬州人在五颜六色的纸或丝缎上剪刻花纹来庆祝节日;唐代,质量很高的贡纸大量生产,剪纸业获得高度发展;清代,扬州经济发达,讲究穿戴,尤其喜欢刺绣服饰,而这些绣品设计就是以剪纸为底样。中华人民共和国成立后,剪纸艺术同其他传统手工艺一样受到政府的重视,2007年成立了**中国剪纸博物馆**⑥,大力促进了扬州剪纸业的发展。

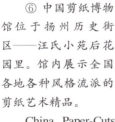

⑥ 中国剪纸博物馆位于扬州历史街区——汪氏小苑后花园里。馆内展示全国各地各种风格流派的剪纸艺术精品。

China Paper-Cuts Museum lies in the back garden of the Wangs' Residence in the historical block of Yangzhou. The museum exhibits a variety of styles and genres of paper-cut artistic treasure all over the country.

In the Sui Dynasty, the people in Yangzhou would cut colorful paper or silks and satins to celebrate festivals. In the Tang Dynasty, the paper-cutting industry became highly developed and a large amount of high-quality paper-cuts were made as presents to the Court. In the Qing Dynasty, due to economic development, the people of Yangzhou became interested in wearing fine clothing, especially embroidered clothing. The embroidered designs were based on paper-cuts. After the founding of People's Republic of China，the Chinese government accepted the importance of paper-cutting like many other arts and skills. In 2007，The Chinese Paper-Cuts Museum opened to the public，greatly promoting the development of Yangzhou Paper-Cutting.

扬州剪纸题材广泛，尤以四时花卉见长，形成了特有的艺术魅力，为中国南方民间剪纸艺术的代表之一。

Yangzhou paper-cutting covers a wide range of subjects，in particular the flowers of the four-season. It forms a unique artistic charm and is one of the representatives of folk arts in southern China.

四 其他手工艺品 Others

扬州玉器 Yangzhou Jade Ware

扬州玉器是汉族民间雕刻艺术之一，扬州是我国玉器重要产地之一。扬州的琢玉工艺源远流长，可追溯到 4 000 年前的夏代。唐代扬州琢玉，在手工业兴盛中有新的发展。清代，扬州成为全国玉材的主要集散地和玉器主要制作中心之一。

Yangzhou is one of the important places for producing jadeware in China. Jade-carving technology has a long history which can be traced back to the Xia Dynasty 4,000 years ago. During the Tang Dynasty，Yangzhou jade carving improved in quality due to the flourishing handicraft industry. In the Qing Dynasty，Yangzhou became the main distribution center of jade and the production center of jade articles.

扬州玉器产品既有雕琢精致的小物件，也有华贵的大型作品，分为炉瓶、人物、花鸟、走兽、仿古、山子雕 6 个类别，品种齐全，花色繁多。扬州琢玉师尤为擅长大型作品，清宫中重达千斤、万斤的近 10 件大玉山，多半为扬州琢制。值得一提的是珍藏在北京博物院的大型玉雕《**大禹治水**⑦图》，高 2.24 米，宽 0.96 米，重达 5 300 公斤，展示了中国琢玉大师的高超技艺。

⑦ 大禹治水是古代的汉族神话传说故事。大禹是黄帝的后代，是中国古代最有名的治水英雄。

King Yu combating the flood was an ancient Chinese myth. Yu, the Great, was the descendant of the Emperor Yellow and a famous hero to control a great flood.

Yangzhou jade products include both exquisitely carved small articles and magnificent large pieces. They are divided into 6 types including bottles, characters, flowers and birds, beasts, simulation of old styles and *shanzi* carving with complete varieties and colors. The largest jade carvings in the Qing Dynasty Palaces were mostly from Yangzhou carvers. What is worth mentioning is the huge jade carving in the Palace Museum in Beijing. It is called *Da Yu Harnessed Flood*, which is 224 cm in height, 96 cm in width, and about 5,300 kg in weight. It is indicative of the high skill of Chinese carving artists.

扬州漆器 Yangzhou Lacquerware

扬州漆器是中外驰名的中国传统工艺产品,不仅外观精美,且耐高温、防潮、防腐。扬州漆器起源于战国;兴旺于秦汉,鼎盛于明清。

Yangzhou Lacquerware is Chinese traditional product and handicraft which is well known both domestically and abroad. Besides just being a pretty sight for the eyes, Yangzhou lacquerware is also impressively resistant to heat, moisture, and corrosion. Originating during the Warring States period, Yangzhou lacquerware flourished during the Qin and Han Dynasties and prospered during the Ming and Qing Dynasties.

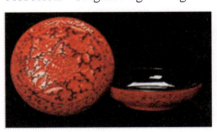

漆器产品用途广泛,如碗、盘、屏风、小装饰盒、桌子和其他家具等。其装饰纹样大量摹刻

"扬州八怪"等名人书画,更提高了扬州漆器的艺术欣赏价值。

The lacquerware products can be used in a diversity of places, like bowls, trays, screens, small decorative boxes, tables and other furniture. The celebrated Eight Eccentrics of Yangzhou also had their calligraphys and paintings etched into lacquer products, which improved their arts value.

现在,扬州生产的漆器产品有屏风、杯垫、椅子、橱柜等三百多个品种。它们既是珍贵的艺术品,又是耐用的实用品。目前,扬州漆器已远销 50 多个国家和地区。2006 年,该技艺经国务院批准列入第一批国家级非物质文化遗产名录。

Today, Yangzhou lacquer products are made into over three hundred different forms, including huge standing partitions, coasters, chairs, liquor cabinets and so on. They are not only precious artworks but also durable and practical articles. Yangzhou exports this little gem in great numbers to over 50 nations. In 2006, the technique was listed in the first batch of national intangible cultural heritage by the State Council.

秦淮灯彩 Qinhuai Lantern

灯彩,又叫"花灯",是起源于中国的一种汉族传统民间手工艺品。它与流传汉族民间的元宵赏灯习俗密切相连。据考证,元宵赏灯始于西汉,盛于隋唐,明清尤为风行。

Lantern making, also named the festival lantern, is a traditional folk handicraft which originated in China. It is closely connected with the traditional custom of making lanterns during the Lantern Festival, which is popular with the Han people. According to research, the custom of creating lanterns for the Lantern Festival originated in the Western Han Dynasty, flourished in the Sui and Tang Dynasties and became popularized in the Ming and Qing Dynasties.

秦淮灯会是流传于南京地区(古称"金陵")的特色民俗文化活动,又称"金陵灯会",主要在每年的春节至元宵节期间在南京夫子庙举行。秦淮灯会源远流长,享有"秦淮灯彩甲天下"之美誉。秦淮灯会的历史最早可以追溯到魏晋南北朝时期,唐代时得到迅速发展,明代时达到了鼎盛。

Qinhuai Lantern Fair, also known as Jinling Lantern Fair, is a popular folk custom celebration of the Lantern Festival in Nanjing area. It is held yearly at the Confucius Temple in Nanjing from the Spring Festival to the Lantern Festival. Honored as the best under heaven, Qinhuai Lantern Festival has a long history going back to the period of Wei, Jin and the Southern-Northern Dynasties. It rapidly developed in the Tang Dynasty and reached its peak in the

Ming Dynasty.

2006 年,秦淮灯会经国务院批准列入第一批国家级非物质文化遗产名录。

In 2006,the Fair was listed in the first batch of national intangible cultural heritage by the State Council of China.

南通蓝印花布 Nantong Blue Calico

南通蓝印花布[8]印染工艺遍及中国江苏南通市的大部分地区。南通民间蓝印花布始于明代,流传至今。现代的蓝印花布主要用于日常衣物、蚊帐、枕套、行李布等。

Nantong blue calico printing and dyeing has been practiced for centuries in most parts of Nantong City,Jiangsu Province,China. Nantong blue calico is handed down from the Ming Dynasty. In modern times,blue calico is used to make the daily clothes,mosquito nets,pillowcases,baggage cloth,etc.

南通蓝印花布因其手工印染过程、自然简单的设计而闻名。蓝印花布的图案取自于动物、植物和民间故事,表达人们对未来生活的美好愿望。

It is famous for its hand-made printing and dyeing process, local and simple designs. The patterns on the blue clothes are based on animals, plants and fairy tales to express the good wishes for the future life.

[8] 南通蓝印花布博物馆是中国第一家集收藏、展示、研究、生产、经营为一体的专业博物馆。

Nantong Blue Calico Art Gallery is China's first specialized Museum including collection, exhibition, research, production and management of the traditional artform.

南通风筝 Nantong Kite

风筝起源于中国,是中国传统手工艺品,传统节日娱乐工具,有着 2 000 多年的历史。南通与北京、天津、山东潍坊同为中国四大风筝产地。南通风筝的艺术风格是简朴的造型、高低

音交响的哨笛装置和富丽典雅的工笔彩绘，以独特的音响效果著称。

The kite first originated in China as a Chinese handicraft for festival entertainment. It has a history of over 2,000 years. Nantong, Beijing, Tianjin and Weifang in Shandong Province are China's four largest kite producing areas. The artistic style of the Nantong kite can be generalized as being plain in design, and demonstrating elegance in a brightly colored pattern. However, the greatest characteristic of the Nantong Kite is its whistle, with both high and low pitches.

惠山泥人 Huishan Clay Figurine

惠山泥人,是江苏无锡汉族传统工艺美术品之一,至今有 400 年历史。惠山泥人造型丰满、简练,夸大头部,着重刻画表情,著名作品"大阿福"代表了勤奋、善良、快乐和乐于助人的精神品格。

The Huishan Clay Figurine is a Chinese traditional artistic handicraft in Wuxi, Jiangsu Province, boasting a history of 400 years at least. Huishan Clay Figurines are short in stature, fat with big heads, and their facial expressions are vividly depicted. The well-known "Da A Fu," which represents a hard-working spirit, kindness, happiness and helpful personality.

桃花坞木版年画 Taohuawu Woodblock Print

木版年画⑨是中国历史悠久的汉族传统民间艺术形式,桃花坞年画因曾集中在苏州城内桃花坞一带生产而得名。桃花坞年画源于宋

⑨ 苏州桃花坞年画、天津杨柳青年画、河南朱仙镇年画、山东潍坊杨家埠年画、四川绵竹年画被称为中国五大民间木刻年画。

Taohuawu prints of Suzhou, Yangliuqing prints of Tianjin, Zhuxianzhen prints of Henan, Yangjiabu prints of Weifang, and Mianzhu prints of Sichuan, are known collectively as the five folk New Year wood block prints of China.

代的雕版印刷工艺，到明代发展成为民间艺术流派，清代雍正、乾隆年间为鼎盛时期，主要表现吉祥喜庆、民俗生活、戏文故事、花鸟蔬果和驱鬼避邪等汉族民间传统审美内容。

New Year woodblock printing is a folk art that dates back hundreds of years. Taohuawu woodblock prints are produced mainly around Taohuawu in Suzhou. It originated from block printing in the Song Dynasty，and later became popularized as a folk art genre in the Ming Dynasty. Taohuawu woodblock prints mainly express the folk traditional aesthetic contents such as auspicious and festive themes，folk life，opera stories，flowers and birds，fruits and vegetables，expelling evil spirits and so on.

任务　Tasks

1. 小组活动　Group Work

看图片讨论剪纸有哪些用途。

Look at the following pictures and talk about the uses of paper-cuts.

2. 小组活动　Group Work

玉是中国传统文化重要组成部分。你能说出一些和玉有关的中国成语吗?

Jade is an intrinsic part of Chinese traditional culture. Do you know any phrases or sayings about it?

3. 小组活动　Group Work

传统手工艺是中国文化宝库里的瑰宝,为中国乃至世界都做出了重大贡献。请讨论并谈一谈你最喜欢的手工技艺。

Traditional handicraft is a precious treasure in Chinese national culture，making a great contribution to China and even the world. Please talk about your favorite handicraft.